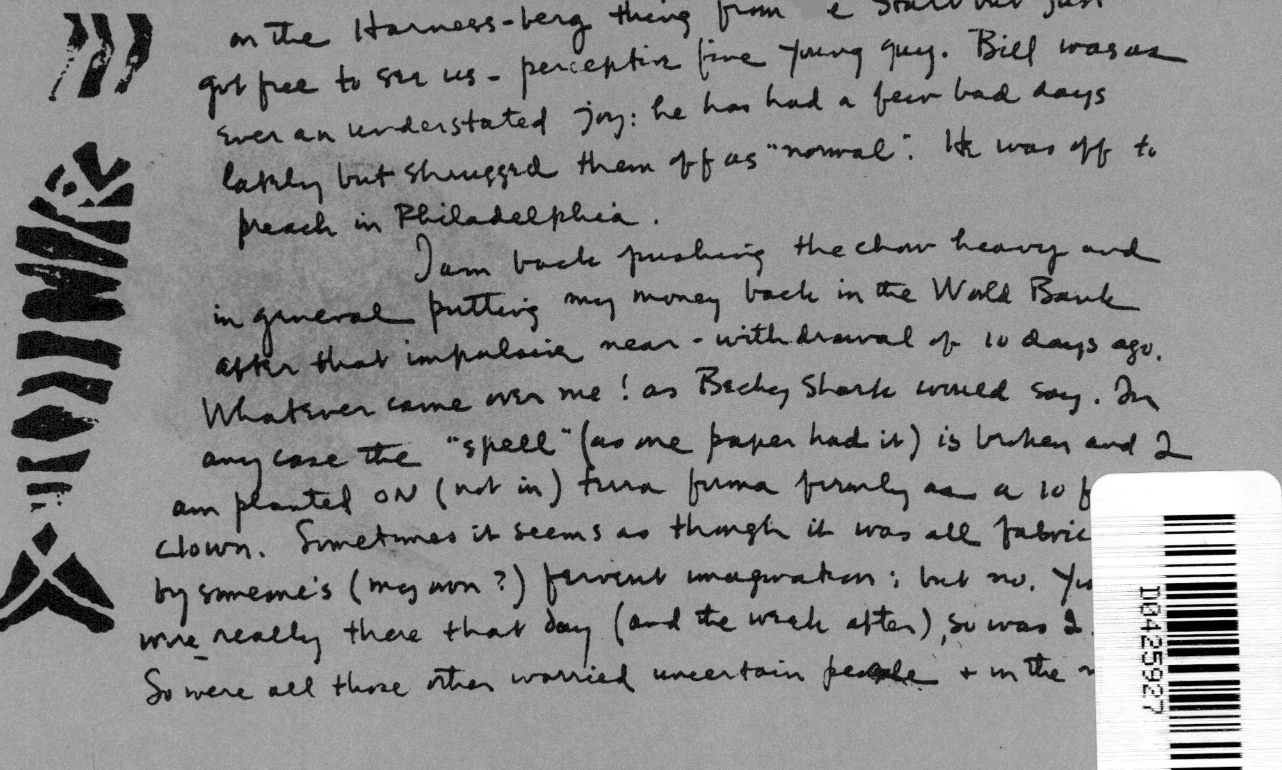
on the Harness-berg thing from the start but just
got free to see us - perceptive fine young guy. Bill was as
ever an understated joy: he has had a few bad days
lately but shrugged them off as "normal". He was off to
preach in Philadelphia.
I am back pushing the chow heavy and
in general putting my money back in the World Bank
after that impulsive near-withdrawal of 10 days ago.
Whatever came over me! as Becky Sharp would say. In
any case the "spell" (as one paper had it) is broken and I
am planted ON (not in) terra firma firmly as a 10 f
clown. Sometimes it seems as though it was all fabric
by someone's (my own?) fervent imagination: but no. Yo
were really there that day (and the week after), so was I.
So were all those other worried uncertain people + in the

America Is Hard to Find

By the Same Author:

Poetry

TIME WITHOUT NUMBER

ENCOUNTERS

THE WORLD FOR WEDDING RING

NO ONE WALKS WATERS

FALSE GODS, REAL MEN

TRIAL POEMS (with TOM LEWIS)

Prose

THE BRIDE

THE BOW IN THE CLOUDS

THEY CALL US DEAD MEN

CONSEQUENCES: TRUTH AND . . .

LOVE, LOVE AT THE END

NIGHT FLIGHT TO HANOI

NO BARS TO MANHOOD

THE TRIAL OF THE CATONSVILLE NINE

THE GEOGRAPHY OF FAITH (with ROBERT COLES)

THE DARK NIGHT OF RESISTANCE

DANIEL BERRIGAN

America Is Hard to Find

DOUBLEDAY & COMPANY, INC.
GARDEN CITY, NEW YORK
1972

ACKNOWLEDGMENTS

Material in this book has appeared in the following publications: *The Christian Century*: "Life at the Edge," copyright © 1970 by Chrsitian Century Foundation. Reprinted by permission from the June 24, 1970, issue of *The Christian Century*. *Commonweal:* "How to Make a Difference," "Notes from the Underground; or I was a Fugitive from the FBI." *Cornell Sun:* "America Is Hard to Find," "maybe the last time . . ." *The New York Times:* "Letter to Judge Roszel Thomsen," copyright © 1970 by The New York Times Company. Reprinted by permission. *The Saturday Review:* "The Passion of Dietrich Bonhoeffer," "The New Man: The 'Compleat Soldier'." *The Village Voice:* "Twice-Born Men: The Unmasking of Fear," "Letter to the Weathermen," reprinted by permission of *The Village Voice*, copyrighted by The Village Voice, Inc., 1970, 1971.

ISBN: 0-385-00327-7
Library of Congress Catalog Card Number 72-76120

Printed in the United States of America
First Edition

CONTENTS

INTRODUCTION

In his essay "Books and Men," Martin Buber speaks of coming to find more in man "to love than to revere." "Man," he says, "is of the world, while books are of the spirit." Books may be read and savored but only for a time—they are of the "other world." Meantime, this world, the "world of men," awaits.

Looking back now to the first spring days of 1970, I get a sense of Buber. He surely would have known what Dan Berrigan was about. For Dan, my brother, writer at that time of a dozen books, had long since "opted" for men.

On the Cornell scene he sauntered briskly and slowly. His style conveyed it: "Want to rap?" What he was saying to people was, "Let's share each other. Maybe we can raise some questions about our lives. Maybe we can enjoy ourselves doing it."

Dan's *esprit* can be put in a word he was then favoring: "Let's *re-member* each other." And the grin, an invitation. His was a sort of concave presence: openings, offerings, welcomes. His hand reached for yours.

As April of that year began Dan was not standing around, though he knew the government, so to speak, had him in mind. "Now comes the hour, Father Berrigan. Surrender. Pay us coin on your debt to society. Requite your criminal act, your burning of draft files. Be a gentleman. Do the decent thing." But Dan had a problem. He knew well that the American government continued to burn children in Vietnam even during those days of his own jeopardy. "Burning of paper" jeopardy, you might call it. Dan questioned government "decency."

One day Dan, my wife Carol and I walked slowly through an Ithaca park. As he often did Dan spoke of people he loved: students, clergy, faculty. "I've been saying goodbye." Then it came, quietly, "My friends want me to resist going to jail. They think I should hide for a while and see what happens."

For Carol and me no more details, only that. For Dan, an attempt, a trial, an essay. Tentatively, out-of-group rappings, sharing, communal insights. No ego trips. Simply, the world of men and Dan of it and in it, freely in jeopardy, taking new directions, inviting new possibilities.

Weeks later Dan, during an "underground" interview, offered a loose rationale for the stance he had come to. "American legal processes are hardly discretionary. Under them there's no provision for moral anguish, moral conviction, moral resistance. No, it's the old story of law hardening, scrubbing itself of human concerns, becoming sterile like the 'facts' it concerns itself with. There's little impartial justice around. Law has become its own end. So why should I submit to those processes? They certainly have nothing to do with me and they're a whole foreign country to where today's resisters are. Not only that but those 'consequences' I'm supposed to have evaded are really there, you really suffer them. For me 'consequences' are loneliness and separation: from family, friends, community." And then came the inevitable paradox that anyone who wants to probe Dan Berrigan's head must expect. "Seems to me that 'consequences' are suffered today by any man who tries simply to become a man." Gently. "Does that make sense?" Beyond Buber to Berrigan.

An overture to Dan's going-under came a week after his descent. At Cornell, "America Is Hard to Find" was a two-day celebration, a healing of head and heart. Following it Dan was under the greensward for sure, trailing behind him hope and laughter and red-faced federal agents thrashing in the dark.

For the family in Syracuse: Mama, Carol, our four kids, me, life went on with some banked curves, some dead ends, to be sure. Respectable church officials avoided us, as did respectable civic officials. But for us the clichés "thin ice," "tightrope," "fear," "risk" had almost no reality, though the dashing on us of hard events sometimes made reflection a surface thing. Still, we came to some sense of the lives of exposed and powerless people in Southeast Asia. This awareness we talked about: those people whose way of life was forced submission to the preemptories of American bombings, strafings, napalmings. In ourselves we tried to gain a sense of the Vietnamese wound. Occasionally we fasted. Our friends loved and supported us. The federal patrol on our street, the phone taps and surveillance all together could not seem to smother our hearts. We did not cease to hope.

Then on a late May day came a phone call from Mama's old friend, Mrs. English. "Jerry, can you come? Your mother has fallen . . ."

So Mama went to St. Joseph's Hospital and our friend Harold Weichert who inserted the conventional pin into her hip told us, "The FBI want me to watch for Dan coming here to see Frida and let them know."

We quickly found there was co-operation in that hospital, but not between the staff and the Berrigans. Once, at the nurses' station I asked, "Can Mrs. Berrigan have a commode by her bed? She finds herself unable to use a bedpan." Four or five times I went there. For my trouble there was puzzlement, incredulity, hostility. But never a commode. And once for half an hour, a night aide taunted Mama who had asked, "Will you please help me to the bathroom?" Gentle Frida, aged eighty-four, was learning hard usage from Christians of patriotic bent. Carol and I were learning with her.

Outside the room where Mama lay, surrounded by three female roommates, watchful feds paced. The whisper drifted in, "How is Mrs. Berrigan? Is she dying?" Mama stirred. We asked, "Does the hip hurt? How about some water? Want the nurse?" She was not plaintive. "Oh Jerry, take me out of this hospital. They don't want me here." Ah but the feds do, Mama, we said to ourselves. The feds want you here because they want Dan *there*. Mentally, we held our wrists together.

Later when Mama's unknit bones required a second, and then a third operation, she was very direct. "Jerry, promise you'll never send me back to that St. Joseph's!" In every room was a crucifix.

Dan stayed away. Blessedly. For a month feds with crockery faces paced the corridors, strode the waiting rooms, peered in doors and up streets. Collusion with nuns, nurses, administrators. Law 'n' order types, God and flag, heads all together: catch Father Dan and damn those other Berrigans, disloyal, godless people.

Days passed. June. Weekly I phoned or was phoned by Dan. A great heartening bond though a private one. To Carol I conveyed the fact of the calls and the "matter," and, of course, also to Phil who was in Lewisburg, fasting in solitary, witnessing for himself and all of us. But thanks to ATT we had a lifeline, Dan and ourselves. Week by week we said to each other, "We're still in the real world, we're making it!"

After his parole happened Dan was asked if he'd felt any psychological pressure during those days. He replied, "Occasionally in jail but underground, never."

Once on our street a neighbor asked Carol, "Did you see that man watching your house? Do you think he could be a pervert, after our kids?" Replied my wife, "Pervert? No! Feds. Our kids are being watched by the government, for free, as if they were kids of the Kennedys or Nixons. Isn't that wonderful?"

As more time passed and Dan's underground community guided him toward this exit for a sermon, toward that for an interview or a TV taping, our hearts swelled. We saw that the feds simply did not know the mettle of their "quarry" (man). They couldn't imagine his physical and psychical tap roots—of joyous rhythms and gospel simplicity. For all the world these agents were trained techno-products, compleat robots, therefore predictable and therefore vulnerable by their own rules. Dan had said, "If you want to catch fish you must metamorphose into a fish." But this our federal friends could not do. Their *esprit* had a fatal fissure: success. So their peerings and probings were marked by arrogance and hence, by blindness.

By early July I was summoned to defend my PhD research at Syracuse University. That same day I emerged, academe's ultimate credential in hand! Some relief!

At our front door a week later, stood the spruce men. They seemed twins of a sort. Mormon elders? But as I opened to them one flashed a badge. "We're federal agents, Mr. Berrigan. May we come in?" Even as I slowly shook my head I was closing the door. That triggered their programmed spiel, right off the turntable: "Five thousand dollars fine, ten years imprisonment for harboring, abetting . . ." Eventually they drove away.

The lone incident was a type of so much that nagged at us in those days, but mainly we were digging deep. Our old life rhythms: home chores, kid cares, school, visits, vacations gradually seemed part of a pattern that was remote, surreal. Mainly in the place of those rhythms came pulses that were less individual, more a part of us as part of people whose lives were on the edge. To be uncertain about private talk, even in private places; to be low-toned in dialogue, even in public; to cast a wary eye at the rear mirror; to sense traps opening—or closing. Finally, we forced ourselves to ask the question: How to escape paranoia? Answer: ignore what you don't know; enjoy what you do!

We came to discover Dan during those one hundred twenty or so underground days—even as we came to discover ourselves. We saw that he embodied joy because he was free. We learned that for one thing Dan saw the Sermon on the Mount not as a discussion club outline but as a guide for action. "Peacemaking is the game, human and divine. So you go out and make peace." For Dan that had to mean resistance because the warmakers are powerful and often, plausible.

Now as I write in April 1972, Dan has served eighteen months in Danbury, Phil has been through the Harrisburg trial, and Nixon is bombing Hanoi. What will be the lives of our children? All four: Philip, Maria, Jay and Carla went with us to visit Phil at Lewisburg, to visit Dan and Phil at Danbury. Several times. What a fundamental and salutary raising of consciousness for those kids! To have been inside American prisons—to have seen and heard and felt the sick pulse of American society—to have kissed and held the hand of men who, perhaps alone, know the cure. For those four children what implications for their present and future concept of society and family and law! In their own lives to whom will they go for liberation except to the prisoners, and to themselves?

April to August, 1970. From those weeks and events and from the months in prison that followed comes this record of Dan's tiltings at the consciousness of America. It is a record simply, of Dan's payments, freely made, for his share in man's common spirit, common flesh. For myself I know a little now of what he has learned, that those payments are never completed.

JEROME BERRIGAN

To Political Prisoners
and the
Underground
from Danbury to San Quentin

I. Prologue

1. AMERICA IS HARD TO FIND

Hard to find;
wild strawberries swans herons deer
those things we long to be
metamorphosed in and out of our sweet sour skins —
good news housing Herefords holiness
wholeness
Hard to find; free form men and women
harps hope food mandalas meditation
Hard to find; lost not found rare as radium rent free
uncontrollable uncanny a chorus
Jesus Buddha Moses founding fathers horizons
hope (in hiding)
Hard to find; America
now if America is doing well you may expect Vietnamese to
do well if power is virtuous the powerless will not be
marked for death if the heart of man is flourishing so will
plants and wild animals (But alas alas so also vice versa)
Hard to find. Good bread is hard to find. Of course. The hands
are wielding swords The wild animals fade out like Alice's cat's
smile Americans are hard to find The defenseless fade away like
hundred year pensioners The sour faced gorgons remain. . . .
But listen brothers and sisters this disk floats downward a flying saucer
in the macadam back yard where one paradise tree a hardy weed sends
up its signal flare (spring!)
fly it! turn it on! become
hard to find become be born
out of the sea Atlantis out in the wilds America
This disk like manna miraculous loaves and fishes
exists to be multiplied savored shared
play it! learn it! have it by heart!
Hard to find! where the frogs boom boom in the spring twilight
search for the odor of good bread follow it
man man is near (though hard to find)
a rib cage growing red wild as strawberries a heart!

imagine intelligence   imagine peaceable caressing food planting   music making
hands   Imagine   Come in!
P.S.   Dear friends   I choose to be a jail bird (one species is flourishing) in a kingdom of fowlers
Like strawberries   good bread
swans   herons   Great Lakes   I shall shortly be
hard to find
an exotic uneasy inmate of the NATIONALLY ENDOWED ELECTRONICALLY INESCAPABLE ZOO
remember me   I am
free   at large   untamable   not nearly
as hard to find   as America

2. MAYBE THE LAST TIME . . .

Coming in by Slowhawk airlines   Thursday last
        in the changeful mad March weather
maybe the last time   seeing from above
             the burgundian walled empire   O Cornell
     your millennial crevasses & wounds
streaming with human juices   the university riding like time's
galleon
        (that geometric delight   square   lozenge   ovoid)
             her decks laid out by Picasso's or Miró's caliper
her trustees puff cheeked like 16 embodied winds in the old maps
        billowing out the silk sails   an eye-bulging world
        empery
               Faster! Faster!
        the faculty busy as deck boys   sweating like sailors
             caught in a contrary drift out of land sight
        Captain Corson saluting at the main mast heroic
straight boned
        as Alec Guiness in his 9 roles awash to his knees
             in the saucy indenturing seas
        and O students!   making do in steerage   your passage to
(somebody's) new world
               muttering like
             Leroi Jones' crew voyaging out of innocence into
               50 states of Mississippi I fear
        your parents' oranges   fluttering handkerchiefs   tearful
pride
             far behind alas   a mirage of Catholic Spain
andlocked Brooklyn
               Dare I say
 love you I will never recover from that illness congenital
        your warts and smiles   your hair like raccoons
t. bernards shetland
               ponies   flourishing winter pelts

your dogs dogs dogs the uncontrollable squatters and runners
hanging around knowing
a good scene when they smell one
eyes feckless as Huck Finn's or Hunna John's
knowing how real a thing is real estate
A good thing! I will never have done with
my lover's quarrel having known
you Hanoi Catonsville trial by fire jail by choice
a departure point of return
an axis a concentrate
a landscape so beautiful it caught the breath
artists buddhists taoists aquarians impassioned
lovers of inner space My quarrel
I will never have done
My quarrel WHETHER IN THE COURSE OF
HUMAN EVENTS IT IS TOLERABLE
(to you or me or the gate post)
that a single child die
who need not have died that a single man despair
whose claim on life is no less binding that air water
education Great Lakes (Cayuga is a great lake) be
priced beyond
all save death by those who Got There First
that tablets commemorating gratefully the "without
which etcetera aid of the U. S. Dept. of defense"
festoon our (value free) research park
(the lies told by priests and rabbis over dead carbuncular
tammany robbers)
WHETHER IT IS TOLERABLE
that the University its counsels impenetrable as
say heaven or hell
decree; *ROTC to be kept unchanged* and simultaneously
CURW to be rigorously reviewed
My quarrel;
often despairing inwardly over *corruptio optimi*
I am (granted) ignorant as a stone
but you sirs are mad in your main parts
and dead as to main issues

or again hearing the night winds this cruel winter;
we have sown the whirlwind
and again incurably addicted to junk rags and the multiple
rusty forms of that Original Found Object named
hope
say within myself
all thanks to dominations powers and
freaks furies friends;
Thank you Cornell has driven me sane

3. THE NEW MAN: THE "COMPLEAT SOLDIER"

"Mistreatment of any captive is a criminal offense. All persons in your hands, whether suspects, civilians or combat captives, must be protected against violence, insults, curiosity and reprisals of any kind. Leave punishment to the courts and the judges. The soldier shows his strength by his fairness and humanity to the persons in his hands."

—Instructions issued to American soldiers on tour of duty in Vietnam.

I have been a soldier, killer, unjustified murderer of yellow
 people.
I have been to the center of my life
where the animal lives
and the rivers run red with blood.

I have come home now,
to the night I have come, through the village OF DEAD
 children.
through hell
to this night, to you.

listen to me church,
listen to me my friends of the church,
if we are not moved by Song My
nothing will move us.
and not even God will save us from
hell.

—A poem written by a returned Vietnam veteran.

After the Tet holiday attacks in South Vietnam in late January of 1968, the air route from Saigon to Hanoi by way of Vientiane slowly resumed its schedule. The initial flight, after the merciless bombardment of the airstrip of Saigon, was something more than an ordinary airlift of mail and personnel in and out of the enemy ɩpital. It "flew out" the first American airmen to be released in the ɔurse of the war into custody of American peaceniks. So Howard inn and I, aging resisters of no mean experience, spent two nlikely hours in the air corridor between the two capitals, in the ɔmpany of three men hot from the forge of military prison.

Howard Zinn's thoughts and mine were, as we recall, of modest ope. Freedom? We had huddled with the "enemy" in subterranean anoi barrows while iron American fists punished the face of the ty. We had walked through the evidence of American air atrocities the Civil Defense Museum, with its eerie bottles of human organs ıt to ribbons by improved antipersonnel weaponry dumped day ter day on the city. We had spent several hours with the airmen efore their release, discussing our return, its meaning and mode. Ve had permitted the three prisoners to probe and question us, to ɩin whatever confidence they could extend to two unknown and ɔne-weary saviors.

But it was the two-hour flight back to Vientiane that I recall most vidly. Talk, talk, one-way talk, coming our way. Drinks, fueling the e, were served by a stewardess for whom such puddle hops between ɔints of danger were a matter of weekly experience. I remember, at ıe point, the clean-boned, twenty-two-year-old junior officer I sat ith leaning across the aisle toward his two companions. He was king about the relative merits of something or other connected ith their bombers: Navy Air Force *vs.* Army, the difficulty of king off from land strips or carrier decks. His left arm went up ke a boomerang or a sail in a fast wind, to demonstrate a point ɔout relative skills. His point made, the three laughed aloud like hoolboys on unexpected holiday.

Indeed, the mood, easily understood, was something like that of a ınday afternoon ball game in Hoosier, Wisconsin. A bit of shing, a sunny day, somnolence, an hour of rest, an errant ball two catapulted into the high grass of left field, a crushed toad. ɔmething accomplished, something done, they'd earned a night's pose.

After Ben Suc, after Song My, after five years of mounting rational horror, after three Presidents and their words, words, ords, after goodness and innocence and grandeur and domestic olence and decay, finally and perhaps pathetically after Catonsville, may be pardoned for a certain wariness, even a certain necessary hardness, in face of this book, *Casualties of War* by Daniel Lang, and its minor American atrocity, the "Event of Hill 192," a Vietnam incident of November 1966.

The guilty place at least as heavy a burden upon us as do the innocent. The question of this book is not so much how to avenge a raped and murdered Vietnamese virgin as how to deal with her technological and primitive killers, the Americans who in most instances are ready, in sky, on sea or land, to perpetrate such deeds as are recorded here. These are the "casualties" produced by military training; by a concatenation of decisions in the vast majority of which no single man has had any voice, though they may affect his culture, his religion, his schooling, his home; or by the slow wet-rot of brain and heart that claims lonely men for its own, waging as they must a war for which no rationale can be offered and no outcome announced.

The incident of Hill 192 is yet another in a series of war crimes to reach our attention. The facts of the case were drawn in the main from the court-martial of four GIs. Prosecution was initiated by a fifth, who had had no part in the crime. That fifth man (whose identity, along with those of the others, the book conceals for obvious reasons) was a member of a patrol in the tortured Central Highlands of South Vietnam. The patrol was assigned to collect "early warning information" about enemy intentions in the area. Their mission required hardy resources of stamina and skill to penetrate deep into enemy territory during a period in which men would be very much on their own, in which "you could count on the unexpected to happen."

The sergeant in charge of the mission concluded his briefing; his final words were a dumfounding bait. The five were to get themselves a woman "for the purpose of boom boom or sexual intercourse, and at the end of five days we would kill her." The sergeant said "it would be good for the morale of the squad."

Glacially, murderously, inevitably, events transpired according to plan. The march began. They came on the girl in a hut sometime before dawn, asleep with her family. She was routed out, was led along by the patrol, her mouth stuffed with a scarf, her shoulders burdened with the pack of one of the more ingenious among the five. In an abandoned hut some distance from her village she was raped by four of the soldiers. Her cries reached the ears of "Sven

Eriksson," the fifth, who had moved away some distance from the hut, abstaining from any part in the outrage.

After the mass rape, the soldiers departed for a reconnaissance tour. Eriksson entered the hut, fed and reassured the girl, and after a desperate effort to concoct some means of saving her, heard the approach of the returning patrol. He realized in a moment of frenzied despair "that there wasn't a thing in the world I could do for her. It was the hardest decision I've ever had to make, and it couldn't have been the best possible one, or Mao wouldn't be gone today."

Given the spiritual climate created by war, at home and abroad, there could of course be no "best possible decision." Eriksson knew it deep in his bones. He had already been threatened and derided. He had no balls; if he refused to join the bacchanalia, he might easily become a "friendly casualty." Two graves instead of one: the victim and her spotless knight. But to what avail?

The girl's agony and Eriksson's marched forward, like a frozen event recorded on a Greek vase, fired and cooled in time. The girl was dragged off into the brush by "Clark," "his hunting knife hidden in one of his hands." When the defense counsel challenged Eriksson during the court-martial to describe the stabbing, he responded: "Well, I've shot deer and I've gutted deer. It was just like when you stick a deer with a knife—sort of a thud—or something like this, sir."

Every study of guilt is also a study of innocence, inevitably, life being something more than a deer hunt. Even in 1970 men can still hear the cry of a stuck deer. Eriksson is the amplifier of that cry, that animal keening, panting, dying in its native bush. A soldier to be sure, a fighter, a hunter not quite converted to the hunt as a lifelong vocation. His will stood firm, be it noted, even after he had failed to come on a way of saving the doe, even after his life and the lives of his family were threatened by the hunters. Quite a man!

The screw is given another turn. For the hunters are an integrated crew. One of them, an officer to whom Eriksson later told his story in an attempt to get an inquiry going, was a certain Reilly, a Black soldier. As a chilling response to Eriksson's experience on Hill 192 Reilly offered his own story. It had to do with Everyman (Black) in any American city at all (white). His was in fact the simple education of any U.S. Negro in the system that binds him body and soul. His wife, he related, had given birth to their first child on the floor of an Alabama hospital after she had been refused admission to the delivery ward. The father, witnessing the birth of his son, had gone berserk. He had tried to wreck the place, had been arrested and jailed. The name of his eventual recovery room was, quite literally, Vietnam. "By the time I got out of jail, I was saying to myself, 'What's happened is the way things are, so why try to buck the system' . . . Better relax about that Vietnamese girl, Eriksson." "Sven had to do what he did," his wife said later. "If he'd kept quiet, he would have been impossible to live with."

The long, lonely agony of Eriksson was under way, that agony whose inception and course is very nearly the only light to shine upon these sinister pages.

The struggle of Eriksson was, I surmise, a little like the moral journey I followed from Hanoi to Catonsville. Certainly Zinn and I came to realize in the course of our visit to Hanoi that the main issue of our voyage, whatever its merits, was not the ferrying of three pilots to safety and "freedom" out of a jail presided over by an implacable enemy. Compassion toward the victims was only one facet, one attitude to be taken. Compassion must be politically understood. Otherwise such ventures as ours could lead only to the bootless and witless journeys we have witnessed in past months of innocents abroad, the widows and the bereaved beating upon the doors of the bargaining agents in Paris. Or such ventures as ours might even lead to the journey of the righteous and rich toward Hanoi in a jet loaded with Western plunder—Santa and his frozen Christmas dinners. No, another question must be asked. Did the billionaires, the bereft wives of America, know anything of Fort Dix and Captain Levy and Leavenworth and the documented torture of Americans by Americans? Did they know of the phone calls we received in the dead of night shortly after return from Hanoi—calls from prisoners' wives, phoning under interdiction of the Pentagon, to learn something of the fate of their loved ones? Could they realize that the enemy was holding American prisoners as one slight bargaining point in a war that was moving closer to the edge of genocide? Did they know that the American military, according to all available evidence, was treating its own sons with a savagery far beyond any experienced at the hands of the "enemy"?

These were indeed unanswered questions as the war went on. Such a war could hardly educate Americans in the truth that underlay the endless irrational character of the war itself. Indeed, such a war was designed simply to blind and retard the moral sense of the aggressor, to guarantee that his crimes against humanity be multiplied; finally, to bedevil the enemy into crimes of his own in retaliation, in revenge, in defense, in despair. For the fact is crime begets crime, an iron jaw promulgated in such times as ours. It was a law recognized even by so unreconstructed a cold warrior as France's Charles de Gaulle: "When the great powers resort to violence as the ordinary way of conducting their affairs, it is not to be wondered that the lesser powers follow suit."

The powers, big and small, follow suit. But Eriksson threw down his hand. That gesture of the powerless! A single man moved away from the doorway of a hut where an intolerable outrage was in progress. He sat down alone on the grass to one side of the structure; periodically he raised his field glasses to gaze at distant points. "The whole thing made me sick to my stomach. I figured somebody would have to be out there for security, because there were Vietcong in the area."

Eriksson did not save the girl, an agony borne home to him in the months and years that followed the crime. Eriksson: modern man in the raw, anti-hero, or demi-hero, his wits—in literature or in life—no better than the ill times create or allow. Not much of a man, some would say. And still, not a killer, which is, the times being what they are, a very great deal. A powerless man, relatively pure in intention, scattered in his moral resources, on his escutcheon written: "Better a live jackass than a dead lion." He can come on no way of saving others. He is, under the iron, cynical glance of power, utterly powerless. Scrounging about on a savage errand for some way to outwit death, he can come on nothing, whether of surprise, of debate, of moral force, of nonviolent resistance; he is very nearly empty. No way of saving another. Basically and irredeemably decent as he is, life appears to him as a gauntlet of grinning, whoring, itchy-fingered men. They are his peers; they wear the same clothing as he, with all the implications stitched into that cut and jib—a uniform that grows on a man like a new skin, the skin of a predator. And as the skin grows, so do the members; the fingers of his hands grow, too, into a stick of iron that belches fire on summons. An obscene biological charade, the "compleat" soldier, the new man.

The other four, the Four Horsemen, have passed their rites of passage. It is no wonder that they are eager to perform on a distant people those deeds that might (or indeed might not) be forbidden to them at home. But they have come into manhood in the only way known (or in fact allowed) to certain Americans today—scrambling for bucks, heirs to small-town (read also Big-Town) puritan morality, small-town (Big-Town) racism, tax squeezes, having no power, fewer alternatives in a dwindling future, no political illumination from above; reared in a cheerless, mortician-minded religion, the sedulous ape (except in instances of violation of special privilege) of the Big Brother state. There is nothing for these men in "normal" society, neither roots, nor schooling geared to their needs, nor land, nor spiritual hope, nor a frontier against which to set their faces. So they grab finally, or are grabbed by, the military, are washed clean in that baptism of the damned, are inducted, swear their oath to Caesar, are clothed in the new garment.

Eriksson had gone nearly the whole way. But at a certain point he stepped aside. He could buy the bag; he could not buy its consequences. Near the hut, as the girl cried out within, he stood aside, a heretic. He had bought in, but only to a point. The rape and death of the innocent, though they might be the logical and inevitable consequence of war, were too much. It made him sick to his stomach—a good sign, a fairly constant one among the inarticulate, stiff-necked men and women who, for no specially attractive or well-reasoned motives, live and die less badly than most of us today.

Two years after the event of Hill 192 I flew with three Air Force men from Hanoi into freedom. On that flight the three joked like adolescents about their planes, their skills, their capers. They conveyed nothing of the dumb and dogged sense of the truth of things, the complicity and gravity of men up to their necks in death, that marked Eriksson so strongly. And none of the steamy sex starvation that drove the four others, like brutal siege-works, into the body of an unknown girl. No, the Air Force is the *haute bourgeoisie* of the militarized American seventies. Its decisions are clean and meticulous: the planning room on high, the charnel house far below. The Air Force is much like the eagle that is its symbol; even its sex is sublime. One could not have imagined the three officers lining up, like neighborhood kids at a Good Humor cart, for free goodies in front of a hamlet shack. No, Air Force sex too partook of a family affair like dinner after church, its issue the crew-cut godly ditto sons sprung from the loins of ditto fathers.

The lives or fortunes of such men as these have little interest for us, not even the interest men desperately attach to the question of their own survival or the survival of mankind. Which is merely to suggest that the military method of the great powers is finished as a way of making history. Vietnam is the last spasm of its legitimacy, and that legitimacy has sputtered out over the village dump to which we have reduced a proud and ancient culture. The military method is finished. In the case of the infantrymen, death close up, sweat, sex, a hunting knife, the cry of a girl. But death in each case, the death of an innocent as an end of things, the death of the protagonists—the "casualties" implied in the title of this book, those agents of death poking away at the dirty end of a systematized, interlocked chain of murder.

Such faithful and obedient men are of no interest to us, except to prove—dead serious or jesting, drop-outs or War College grads, neutral or religious, ambitious or despairing—the bankruptcy, the burned-out instance of conscience, the debased methods of the military Dispos-All.

Yet my thought returns again and again to that anonymous resister, so like his companions in every way, armed like them, uniformed, trained, obedient. What made the difference, at the icy point of drawn knives? Was it a young wife at home? (But at least two of those who raped and killed were married, and one had a two-year-old daughter.) Was it a kind of simple dogged decency, or what we used to call *pudor*, still uncorrupted by a hot-crotch culture? Was it the freedom from racism that marked his background, Minnesota being in this regard typical of neither the North nor the South, but a homogeneous community of white farm people?

In any case, Eriksson reminds us once more that the future, whatever of it we can claim, is in the hands of heretics. The faithful, whether of Holy Mother State or of Holy Mother Church, are largely finished as types or models. Given the culture, given hot war following upon cold, given technology gone mad as a March hare, given "drop by drop" (the phrase is North Vietnamese) troop removal, given Nixon fixated on football while the half million march by—given ourselves, in sum—Eriksson takes on his real stature. He is the near-hero, the near-saint cast up by the times, the best we have, gifted with that bare minimum of imagination and nerve to see him through, a whole skin, something of a whole conscience. Granted that no great claims can be made for him; still, his quality is rare indeed. By not kidnaping or raping or killing during one day of his life he won through, at his throat the knifepoint of an event that occurred (as the defense put it during the court-martial) not "in civilization, but out on combat operations." No war resister he, no great questioner, neither mystic, intellectual, nor saint, not gifted enough to snatch a girl from violation or death. Not heroic enough to die rather than allow a crime to proceed to its foul and bloody closure.

And yet, given everything, man enough.

About a year and a half after the events of Hill 192, nine of us invaded the draft board at Catonsville, Maryland, extracted some 350 draft files and burned them in a parking lot nearby with homemade napalm. Almost two years after the events of Hill 192, our trial opened in a federal court in Baltimore. Our defense was based on a premise so simple as to be all but unintelligible to our society. After four years of resisting war, and many more years of resisting exploitation, misery and racism, we had taken thought among ourselves. Our conclusion: it was better to burn papers than to burn children.

This was an audacious, arrogant, and finally intolerable form of reasoning, as the loss of appeal will shortly demonstrate. The boxes of paper ash were wheeled into court on the first day of the trial as evidence against us. But the bodies of napalmed children could not be produced; they were abstractions, distant, debatable objects unrelated to the brute facts of the case. Those facts, pressed hard by the government, went as follows: nine men and women, led by whatever capricious demons, ran amok and destroyed government property, holding up before unclean, hairy, drug-ridden, irresponsible crazies of the nation an invitation offered by a group of besotted religious malcontents. "Come on, do as we did. Let's bring the whole thing down."

The facts were, of course, something totally other. Our action was nonviolent, careful of human life and well-being, and proceeded as the outcome of a long and lonely social protest, preceded by years of service to our society. But nothing of this was to the point. The jury, borne aloft in airy platonic weightlessness by the judge's instruction, was allowed to consider only "the facts," apart from all moral or social circumstance: whether we nine, on such and such a date, entered, rifled, and burned with "inflammable material" (the obscene word *napalm* never passed the lips of prosecutor or judge) certain properties of the United States Government, valued in excess of one hundred dollars.

Inevitably, the event of Hill 192 casts a cruel light on the nature of such government properties. For the papers destroyed at Catonsville in May of 1968 were in fact hunting licenses issued against human beings, licenses declaring a twelve-month open season on Vietnamese men, women, and children. Hill 192, Song My, the wasting of Hanoi and Haiphong from the air, and in South Vietnam a massive daily assault on ecology and populace—all are articulated phases in a single strategy, filed and legitimatized in the airless shabby offices of American draft centers. The court-martial of four enlisted men who kidnaped, raped, and killed an unknown Vietnamese girl was in no sense meant as a deterrent against such crimes as this. Rather, the legal proceedings served, as Eriksson seemed to realize, only as a charade of justice behind which the most atrocious crimes ensue. Here and there enlisted men, generally cowed by a misbegotten system, sexually starved, lonely, spiritually adrift, pure American products, disposable items to be used and thrown away—such men as the Hill 192 four—pay a price for going to war.

Not so heavy a price, either, as things turned out. Of the four court-martialed soldiers two are already at large, and the sentences of the remaining two have been reduced again and again. From this and other instances it becomes clear that military justice acts as a public pacifier, quelling the first storm of outrage, and is in no sense related to civilized justice.

No such sunny prospect as a reduction of sentence awaited the Catonsville felons. Two crimes: the burning of hunting licenses issued against humans, and the hunting and slaying of human beings. War, which institutionalizes the second, must with utmost rigor punish the first. Simply translated, the Catonsville nine will undoubtedly spend a longer time in prison than the Hill 192 four.

But even the slight and symbolic punishment meted out in wartime to rapists and murderers never threatens those whose decisions make such crimes inevitable. The Nuremberg Code, whatever its merits, is a dead letter. And it is just such contraventions as the Vietnam War or, more properly, American military and political power that have struck it down. In remote board rooms, far from crime or punishment, that power moves majestically on its way, in accord with its own ends, methods, and timetable. And literally no one declares to the American mandarins—executive, military, judicial, or legislative—how far is too far; no one sets limits or imposes penalties on this monstrous, self-regulating inflation of human power.

Moreover, no one (and here we touch the nerve of the tragedy), no one offers to power a vision or a new way. Those of us who are powerless must literally make do with a few Erikssons, a few resisters, a few draft-file burners, with semi-heroes and anti-heroes. No one of us, nor all of us taken together, can save the victims. Our profitless task is our "No," uttered at the shabby door of a civilization where today and tomorrow the rape of the innocent is in progress, and murder is the hourly outcome.

4. A LETTER HOME FROM CORNELL

Wed. P.M.
March 1970

Dear Mama,

This AM we received confirmation of rejection of our appeal by the Supreme Court. I talked to Carol & to Jim & Rosalie (Jerry was out) this evening. They told me you had heard the news, and also that you knew we now have 30 days before prison. So I don't have to fear; you are very well prepared and courageous as ever we knew you.

If I have any regrets they circulate around Pa not living to share this new honor to his 2 sons and priests. But you are with us for the greatest days we have known—to be in jail in protest against the destruction of innocent life in a senseless and savage war, without issue, meaning or outcome. I thank God with all my heart that He spared you for these days at our side. Your prayers and courage our best support.

I wanted you to have Fr. Shea's letter. It seems remarkable to me that he understands so well what Phil and I are trying to say.

Much love and hope, and I will see you Sunday. We are on the edge of great honor, and the gratitude of good men and women everywhere. You are in our hearts.

Daniel

II. Underground

1. LETTER TO THE JESUITS

April 10, 1970

Dear Father General, Father Provincial, and Brothers in Christ:

This week marks the anniversary of the deaths of Dietrich Bonhoeffer (1945) and of Teilhard de Chardin (1955). It is the week in which the felons of Catonsville are summoned by the state to begin their prison sentence. In such circumstances, I wish with all my heart to write the brethren. For it is my intention, as well as that of my brother, to provoke another crisis in our long struggle with the United States war in Vietnam.

Philip and I, priests of the church, intend this week to resist the automatic claim on our persons announced by the U. S. Department of Justice. We believe that such a claim is manifestly unjust, compounded of hypocrisy and the repression of human and civil rights. Therefore only one action is open to us: to declare ourselves fugitives from injustice. For we are not criminals; our action at Catonsville harmed no one; the property we destroyed was an abominable symbol of idolatrous claim on human life.

We are not criminals, but we choose to be exiles in our own land.

Two years after Catonsville, the arguments we proposed against the slaughter of the innocent go unheeded. Our government widens the swath of death in Southeast Asia. Indeed, as the trial of our brothers and sisters in Washington, and the pretrial orders of the judge of the Chicago Fifteen both declare, the courts have stopped their ears against our cry for justice and peace. It is now officially forbidden under threat of heavy penalty to initiate public debate on the issues which our acts have striven to raise. We are gagged in public and in the courts. And a war, undeclared and in despite of every humane and constitutional law, goes on like a runaway nightmare.

In the face of such events, the courts have become more and more the instruments of the warmakers. Can Christians, therefore, unthinkingly submit before such powers? We judge not. The "powers and dominations" remain subject to Christ; our consciences are in his keeping, and no other. To act as though we were criminals before God or humanity, to cease resisting a war which has immeasurably widened since we first acted, to retire meekly to silence and isolation—this seems to Philip and me a betrayal of our ministry. In my own case, it seems a betrayal of my love for the Society.

My thought in these hours is above all for the brethren. No one of us needs to be told that the times are such as to bring despair to all but the strongest. There are Jesuits who, almost like lemmings, look with deadly equanimity to the dissolution of the Society. There are others who assess their chances—here or there—church or world—as though to pass from life into American culture were no more than the cool trading of one profession for a more promising one. Such men have found no serious reason for remaining in the brotherhood; many of them find no significant place in the world. Inevitably, they taste ashes in their mouths, in both places.

But at this point of my life, I have no heart for entering upon debate or analysis. My own hope at this point remains firm. I hope that at least a minority of the brethren may remain together in the years ahead, to form a confessing brotherhood—a community in which men may speak the truth to men, in which our lives may be purified of the inhuman drives of egoism, acculturation, professional pride, and dread of life. A brotherhood which will be skilled in a simple, all but lost art—the reading of the gospel, and life according to its faith.

The American church knows little of such realities. Many of our leaders are effectively inoculated against Christ and his Spirit. Many of them spend their lives in oiling the ecclesiastical machinery, and on Sundays conduct the White House charades that go by the name of worship. Nothing, literally nothing, is to be expected from such men, except the increasing suffocation of the Word, and the alienation of the passive from the realities before us.

No, we must begin again, where we live. The real question of the times is not the conversion of cardinals or presidents, but the conversion of each of us.

There are few American Jesuits who, if their speech is to be trusted, are unaccepting of change. Most of us are obsessed with its inevitability. We talk persuasively of it, we grasp at new forms and styles. And yet the suspicion remains; very few of us have the courage to measure our passion for moral change against the sacrifice of what lies closest to our hearts—our good name, our comfort, our security, our professional status.

And yet, until such things are placed in jeopardy, nothing changes. The gospel says it; so do the times. Unless the cries of the war victims, the disenfranchised, the prisoners, the hopeless poor, the resisters of conscience, the Blacks and Chicanos—unless the cry of the world reaches our ears, and we measure our lives and deaths against those of others, nothing changes. Least of all ourselves; we stand like sticks and stones, impervious to the meaning of history or the cry of its Lord and Victim.

I do not wish to preach a homily. I wish to send a word of love to the brethren, who have been for these thirty years my bloodline, my family, my embodied tradition and conscience.

For you as well as for my own manhood (believe me, it is a word of love) I do not hesitate to be found anathema before the state. I refuse to rest easy in the niche of a benign and complaisant man—by which image my friends make bearable my imprisonment. I refuse, under a simple logic, to be so disposed of; if our political leaders were true to their mandate and the war were ended, my imprisonment would be a manifest absurdity (and probably would never occur). But since public policy goes its monstrous and desperate course, I must be hunted down and "punished."

Before that threat, I can only resist. Granted that my act of resistance is no more than symbolic (I have no desire to become the prey of an open hunting season on human beings).

Therefore in the future, when my point is made and the good of the community has been served, I shall surrender to Caesar. But the time and place will be my own; his embarrassment will pay tribute to my freedom.

But for us, the abiding question has nothing to do with Caesar. The abiding question is the meaning and direction of our lives. I offer you only a sign, one man's choice, in the hope that my life may serve yours. During the seminar at

Woodstock, N.Y., during the past winter, our discussion on the new man was often heated and anguished. No one of us who took part in those evenings came away without the sense, obscure but unfailing, that our birth in the spirit awaited a new acceptance of the world, with all that implied: moral crisis, infamy, risk, obloquy, mistakes, *horror vacui,* misunderstanding, the ability to deal with personal and social violence, the breakup of cherished hope, the tearing apart of even the most admirable cultural fabric. The loss of all things, in fact: "if only Christ be gained."

A virile faith does not allow the times to snatch from us what we are invited to give. Our lives included. I ask your prayers, that my brother and I, and all who are at the edge, may be found faithful and obedient; in good humor, and always at your side.

Daniel Berrigan, S.J.

2. THE PASSION OF DIETRICH BONHOEFFER

I begin these notes on 9 April 1970. Two hours ago, at 8:30 A.M.,
I became a fugitive from injustice, having disobeyed
a federal court order to begin
a three-year sentence for destruction of draft files two years ago.
It is the twenty-fifth anniversary of the death of Dietrich Bonhoeffer
in Flossenbürg prison, for resistance to Hitler.
The temperature outside is 64. It is a foggy, wind-driven day
well tempered to my mood.
But let me begin at the beginning.
My theme, as Bonhoeffer would put it, is faith and obedience.
He said: *Invisibility breaks us to pieces.* Again:
Simply suffering; that is what will be needed—not parries or blows
or thrusts. The real struggle which perhaps lies ahead
must consist only in suffering belief.
And again: *The task is not only to bind up the victims beneath*
the wheel, but also to put a spoke in that wheel.

I came to this place thirty-six hours ago, a decision of a few friends and
myself. My family being powerless in this instance
to help, the Jesuits unwilling.
Came to this house, receiving from the first moment such welcome
as all outdoors presaged: the streams running free
the hill shedding like behemoth its polar coat.
A man, a woman, a child; forsythia at the kitchen table
the old house anchored 100 years to its hillside;
a tree older than the house, big as a household god (fifty years ago
a former slave climbed the hill every year, they say, to measure it).

Bonhoeffer! The book by his friend Eberhard Bethge
required five translators from the German; no less. An elephantine
delivery, slow in the issue, portentous in the outcome.
A German processional elephant; Bonhoeffer riding, not gracefully
but, one judges, quizzically, accepting
(he was a miracle of acceptance) this palanquin-like passage;

hundreds of footnotes; the endless conferences, mission tours,
youth clubs, gatherings. Churchy stuff! He saw only gradually;
such a game, for bad times, could only be preliminary. One tried
"corporate decisions," one waited
on the awakening of others. But not, God help us, forever!

The iguana was abroad in the night; it was impossible to compose
in advance, scenarios for containing or snaring him.
One day Bonhoeffer realized this.
From that hour he was a dead man—in church and state.
Hitler; clever as only a madman, aided
by the contrary madness of his adversary, and the tacky wind
of chance and mischance, can be. Thus: Churchill's
smoldering fury (smoldering Dresden), the "no surrender,
no quarter given" Allied policy, the old bankrupt tactic of
Versailles, trotted out once more.
For Germans, the issue (dissembled, concealed, misconstrued
with utmost cunning by Hitler): was it possible for the church
to witness its faith, and in consequence, defend
the victims (Jews) even to the point of bringing a like storm upon
Christians also? Was there indeed, such being the times,
an adversary, any other conceivable way of witnessing?
Or was the church
no more than a state function (a White House Sunday morning)?
The state flag its emblem also, the cross bent at its four
extremities, a swastika the murderous sprocket
of Caesar's wheel?
Bonhoeffer was to learn; the theologian must yet
become a Christian, and after that a contemporary. The process
would turn the seams of his mind inside out would draw him very far
(far as prison and death) from conventicles, honors,
a good name in his community, the hope (often a diseased delaying
tactic) for gradualism, for church or state reform.
Obscurely, he saw the issue from the start; and began to pay, from the
start:
"I am working with all my might for church resistance.
But it is perfectly clear to me that this resistance is only
a temporary and transitional phase that will lead on to
opposition of a quite different kind; and that only very

few of the men in this preliminary skirmish will commit
themselves in the next struggle. . . . The whole of Christendom
should pray with us that it will be a 'resistance unto death,'
and that people will be found to suffer it."

This likable learned bourgeois German! He was growing up, in the
saucy intemperate weather of the real world.

Theology
was no impediment, wonderfully. Learning was no deferment.
Research, writing, lectures, libraries: the baggage might break the
back of a man on march. What then?

Rid one's self. Strike free. Live
on the move. He was behaving
as though the storm of tomorrow, gathering, had
already struck. His prophetic bones!

In 1932, Hitler: *The National Socialist Party does not wish to save
the fatherland without the cooperation of the forces
of the church.*

Again, to church leaders: . . . *safeguarding our national heritage.
Christianity, the unshakable foundation of
our peoples' ethical and moral life.*

In February 1933: *We promise to take Christianity, the basis of our
whole morality, under our firm protection.*

Bonhoeffer said publicly: *The image of the leader, should he allow
himself to succumb to the wishes of those
he leads, gradually becomes the image of
the "misleader." This is a leader who
makes an idol of himself and his office,
and thus mocks God.*

Hitler, during the same years, was eroding personal and civil rights. In 1935 he struck most boldly. His "EDICT FOR THE PROTECTION OF THE PEOPLE AND STATE" abolished virtually all rights conceded by the constitution, and thus made concentration camps possible. His "LAW TO RELIEVE THE NEED OF THE PEOPLE AND THE STATE" released him from any dependence on the constitution, should this prove embarrassing. The election of March of that year meant that the majority of the German people accepted, de facto, the end of freedom of the press, of right of public assembly; intervention of privacy in all communication; authorization of enter and search; confiscation and restriction of property.

But Hitler's appeal to the churches
must rank among the cleverest of his moves. By it he hoped
to play the mystagogue, dividing and bewildering the churches on the
basis of loyalty to the state. And more important: to enlist the
churches in the mounting fury of his campaign against the Jews.
In this campaign even "non-Aryan" Christians
were not spared infamy. They were to have
"separate but equal" facilities.

A nightmare is its own legitimation. (So is slavery; so is war; so
is racism, etc. etc.) It is difficult to realize this, to
"imagine the real world." Men are enclosed in the
capsule of events and understanding. And events have a profound
and subtle way of exerting moral change: the pressure of wind on the
rhythms and stance of a tree, of water upon stone. Prior strength
is no guarantee against erosion, crumbling, death.
Thus, the "Jewish question" raised by Hitler is
to decent men no question at all. Yet because it was pushed hard and
fast it took on the sophistic and squalid legitimacy he sought.
What had been in normal times the edgy domain of cranks
suddenly became the hot potato of serious political and (even)
theological debate.
Should Jews be allowed to exist? (Should Blacks be allowed?)
Rubbishy times create a mountain of rubbishy questions.
It is the ecological image of Eliot's "distracted
from distraction by distraction. . . ."
In such times, key questions of decency, justice, peace,
the sharing of the world's goods,
are lost at the bottom of a cosmic dump.
A momentous effort of burning, sifting and removal, if ever
the real questions are to be rescued from the wreckers!

Bonhoeffer burned, sifted, removed. The task of a good man in a bad
time was to despise, to put to naught, the tactics of evil power.
He stepped time and again over the red herrings in his path
holding his nose against their stench. Thus,
To the question of whether the church should connive with the state in
the suppression, deportation and murder of Jews, he proposed a concrete answer: the formation at Finkenwalde, in 1936, of a brotherhood

of young seminarians, to engage in study, discipline and prayer, and (in the event, only known afterward) to prepare for resistance and death.

To the question of Aryan doctrines of blood purity, he proposed over several years the exploration of the Sermon on the Mount as a basis for "worldly Christianity"—*i.e.,* the morally visible and inevitably assailed life of man in a "boundary situation"—with regard both to the Caesarian church and the Caesarian state.

(Our judge let it be known recently
to the Catonsville felons:
once you have surrendered yourselves
and are safely under lock and key
I will call a hearing
and attend to arguments
relative to reduction of your sentences.
Now regarding the question of carrots
held on sticks in front of noses
I am not a passionate vegetarian.
It seems to me a question must be
organically in place
if it is to be a serious question.
The serious question for us
if we are to continue faithful
to the impulse that led us to Catonsville
is not the question of our own welfare
but the moral trajectory of our act—
that it fly undeflected, to the heart of the matter
which is
the infamy of the widening war
the grief torture dislocation death
rape murder terrorism
inflicted by our government
upon the innocent)

Bonhoeffer gathered strength; his stature grew
stubborn with the stubbornness of water
that "lesser strength which explores
the edges and interstices of power"
and comes on a different way.

Political man is a synonym for believing man
(in the beginning he did not understand this).
Perhaps the matter should be put more simply:
political man is the natural term of man, his adulthood.
In such a formula, many converge
(quite naturally without prior agreement
hearing in the air voices beckonings incarnations)
out of intolerable suffering brutalized lives
(themselves, their brethren)
upon one moment, one brotherhood
(one death? maybe.—
one prison? probably)

Toward the end, in the last five years of his life
all the carpetbagging fell behind;
he had raised no intellectual fiefdom
the symbols were all consumed assimilated
he was new bread and wine, reborn!
His reflection and writing and prayer ripened, the natural fruit
of that "life at the edge"—
He encouraged communities of resistance
He lived "in God and with God, as though God did not exist"
which is to say, as though God were indeed God
not score keeper, Band Aid, bonbon, celestial oracle,
Good Humor man.

I think I know the direction of Bonhoeffer's life—even from afar! Sitting on the floor of a bedroom in a country area, curtains drawn, totally dependent on the risk-taking of a few friends, reading and meditating, realizing in one's deepest being how few will understand, speaking the truth even when ears seem turned to stone. I think I understand!

But there is more; and of it one cannot speak as yet, in our case. In Bonhoeffer's, the course is by now clear, and Bethge writes openly of it:

> Any responsible resistance under the conditions Hitler had brought about was bound, strictly speaking, to take the form of conspiracy. A spontaneous rising did not occur and could not be expected to occur; a spontaneous individual action might be brave, but it left out of account one's responsibility for the future; and there were

scarcely the homogeneous lines of approach needed for a revolution
that had the force to throw up a new form of social structure.

By imagining the future, Bonhoeffer helped create it. At Christmas 1942,
he wrote:

> The ultimate question for a responsible man is not how he is to extricate himself heroically from the affair, but how the coming generation is to live. It is only from this question, with its responsibility toward history, that fruitful solutions can come, even if for the time being they are very humiliating.

He came to realize as every legitimate authority was stripped or corrupted
as neighboring countries were ravaged
as Jews disappeared like animals in night-set traps
someone had to take on the shady business!
"Render to Caesar . . ." "Be cunning as serpents . . ." The mind of
Jesus had—how say it?—a worldly twist; the disciple was not to perish
witlessly, without responsibility to others, to the movement.
In June of 1939, Bonhoeffer left Germany for the United States.
No sooner there, he was seized by the deepest anxieties,
could not settle into the work offered him. He must return.
A momentous, wholly correct choice, hindsight. Going
home meant simply: walking into the coils of the protective cobra.
And he was right; he belonged to the confessing church, to the Jews,
to the victims already in concentration camps, to the ghettoized
and brutalized, to the few scattered c.o.'s.
He must continue to confront and unmask the lies; blood and iron,
Aryan purity, Jew perfidy, the S.S., the swastika-draped altars,
the boots and brutes. He was right;
a man belongs with his people, when his people
are ill and power is awry and only a lively tongue and mind
and that courage which is more crucial than intelligence
and (if required)
imprisonment and death
can bring access to health.
On June 22, 1939, he wrote Reinhold Niebuhr:
I have made a mistake in coming to America. I must live
through this difficult time with the Christian people of
Germany. I will have no right to participate in the recon-

struction of Christian life there after the war if I do not share the trials of this time with my people. . . . Christians in Germany will face the terrible alternative of either willing the defeat of their nation in order that Christian civilization may survive, or willing the victory of their nation and thereby destroying our civilization. I know which of these alternatives I must choose; but I cannot make that choice in security.

He returned to Germany after only one month, though his visit had bee
arranged for a year. Nor could he ever say precisely
why he returned; though he was reportedly quite clear
as to why he left Germany.
Indeed he had set down, in his usual precise fashion,
Three reasons for that last-minute voyage from his homeland (a voyage
which he never dared call a flight).
1-2-3. The reasons were persuasive to him at the time.
(They were invalidated in one month.)
1) to relive the isolation of the church 2) to vindicate the freedom of the church for special missions 3) to avoid the draft.
They were "churchy" reasons, selfish reasons. They involved the well-being
of a structure, proving something (as well as saving his own skin).
He returned. And he came to this decision for no reason at all,
as such things are commonly understood. No reason. Existence. Fidelity.
The spirit. Destiny. Folly. Whatever it is
draws men and women out of the common rut of rationality and at the same time
hides from them every vindication, proof,
the lying clarity of the conscious mind.
He wrote at the time: *It is strange I am never quite clear about the motives that underlie my decisions.*
He meant the real ones.
He had been clear about leaving Germany; then he was right.
That gave pause. He came home, humbled; *simply because*
that is where our life is; and because we abandon, destroy our life
if we are not back in the fight.

April 10, 1970, Friday. Anniversary of the death of Teilhard.
A stormy petrel of a day. As though a tranquil page had turned back

under a contrary draft of wind.
A mood of peace, of rightness, all the horrors and honors at some distance. I feel strongly suspended in mind.
The gently anchoring fact is the presence of my friends—
their courtesy, their ease and acceptance.
I sit here alone with a dog in an old farm kitchen
very like the one of my boyhood.
The heavy winds put shoulder to the house.
There are pails and boots and jackets about,
signs of a land lying close to the door sill.
My life has anchored in a great simplicity.

Bonhoeffer went to almost any length to save important men; Niemöller was urged to volunteer for the navy, after war broke out in 1939. Bonhoeffer himself applied to become a military chaplain.
Finally he entered upon the most perilous phase of his life. He joined in a conspiracy to assassinate Hitler, in order to bring down the Third Reich, and open the way for negotiations with the Allies.
Now presupposing, as I firmly believe, that the Vietnam war is comparable in its genocidal character to Hitler's war and his near
extinction of the German Jews, one asks himself
whether Phil and I would at this stage, or any immediate future
stage (or indeed at any point in the past four years), venture in any such direction.
We would not, by any means.
Which is not to say: we condemn this good man. Only to say
we have learned from him, from Hitler, from Johnson and Nixon
and the German church and the American church
from the cold war and the nuclear arsenals
from the flareup and quick demise of student movements
perhaps most of all from one another
what for us here and now are the limits of equivocal gesture.
The gradual growth of heroic understanding, in Bonhoeffer's case
is thrust at us more quickly, a kind of forced growth
from the brutal and unpredictable American experience.
We stand with Bonhoeffer, whose struggle
was more protracted, who was faithful unto death.
We, too, wish to be both Christian and contemporary. And this accounts,
paradoxically, for the difference between us and him.

Toward the end, in Tegel prison, tenderness and joy
descended upon him. It was not that conditions became less horrible.
But his superspy cloak and dagger existence
fell away like a rotten garment.
He became engaged to marry, an astonishing
act of faith, a leap into the unknown. A man of thirty-seven
eminent in his life and works
but living under a heavy cloud, a prisoner of the state
whose life is soon to be forfeit
engages himself to an eighteen-year-old girl.
His fiancée visited him unexpectedly;
it was their first and last meeting
in the whole course of his imprisonment.

On April 2, 1945, Bonhoeffer said to a fellow prisoner that *it was his duty not only to comfort the victims of the man who drove in a busy street like a menace, but also to try to stop him.*

John Hogan, at the Catonsville trial, said:

If there were a group of children
walking along the street
returning home from school
and a car
came down the street
out of control
If I could divert the car
from crashing into those children
I would feel an obligation
to turn the car from its path.
It is possible something would happen
to the individual in the car.
But no matter. I would be thinking
ten times more of those children.

Bonhoeffer was finally executed on 9 April 1945. Sometime later, his parents wrote to a friend:

"You know that we have been through a lot and lost two sons and two sons-in-law through the Gestapo. For years we had the tension caused by anxiety for those arrested, and for those not yet arrested but in danger.

But since we were all agreed on the need to act, we are sad, but also proud of their attitude, which has been consistent."

* * *

I am responsible, not to the warmakers and purveyors of violence, but to the community of peacemaking resistance.

16 April 1970

3. A LETTER FROM THE UNDERGROUND

April 24, 197
Fri. PM

Dear Mamma,

A brief note to say hello. The past days as you undoubtedly have been sharing them, have been quite hectic. We were all distressed by Phil's sudden arrest. I had had a few days with him prior to this so was somewhat more resigned. The main thing is that he went in good spirits and for a good cause. So there is no reason to be dismayed. Really we have all been facing these things for so long now that regret or second thoughts are of no moment.

I wish there were more to report from my point of view. I have decided with the help of friends to keep free for a time yet. It remains to be seen how long this will be borne with by those in authority, but we will try. I am in excellent health and spirits, mean as ever really, and buoyed up by your good wishes and prayers which I know are always at our side.

Someone said Jerry was in NY to visit Phil and I was sorry to miss that opportunity. I have had a few good newspaper interviews—everyone seems interested in our plight—and have been doing plenty of meditating and study and even a bit of writing.

Please give my love to Jerry and Carol and the Rizzo's and all our friends. I heard Rosalie left for the Virgin Islands so you will have to convey our best wishes in that direction.

Could not be in better health, and think of you so much. *And* of course thanking God for your great *SPIRIT!*

Love,
Danie

4. FROM THE UNDERGROUND #1

On April 21 at 5:30 in the afternoon in New York City, my brother Philip and another war resister were dragged from a Catholic priests' residence by agents of the FBI. Thus, abruptly, the two began serving federal prison sentences (of six and three years respectively) for destruction of draft records.

Eight Catholics, including Philip and myself, have been sought by federal authorities since April 9, the date set for our surrender. That surrender was considered practically a foregone conclusion. Were not three clerics involved? And even if clerics, in a passing fit of aberration, had once chosen to disobey the law, would they not now choose to repair their crimes with due promptitude? Indeed was not the Catholic Church, to which they professed adherence, the greatest single supportive force of the Vietnam War, outside the government itself?

Indeed yes. The government was so sure of its prey that it even let us know some days before our surrender date that its justice would be tempered by mercy. Once we were safely behind bars, a hearing on reduction of our sentences would be held; the outcome, it could be expected, would be benign. Thus the whip and the carrot, in judicious combination, were to keep our skittish spirits pacified.

But on April 21, in New York, that plan was formally abandoned as useless. No more threats, no more rewards. Some one hundred federal agents invaded the rectory of St. Gregory's Church, battered down doors, and led the two resisters away. The police widened the cast of the net to include a Catholic convent in the same area. For two successive days they entered and searched every corner in pursuit of your correspondent. Obviously, they did not come upon him.

This happy phenomenon may bear some reflection: how is it that, having chosen to break a law and thereby presumably suffer the consequences, one is led further into an obscure twilight existence, neither prison nor freedom, somewhere between crime and punishment? Is it realistic in such a nation as ours, where revolutionary rhetoric is common and revolutionary conditions have by no means coalesced (even in the case of Black Panthers), that a white cleric, sprung from a culturally stifled church, unfailingly obedient to Caesar, should now hear a different drummer, and fall in? Is the term "underground," as applied to the American instance, a will-o'-the-wisp? What, in America, differentiates the moral witness of a jailed man (like my brother) from an invisible man (like me)? What can actually and usefully be done now, in my circumstances, for the peace movement?

There is a mythology abroad in our country, sedulously fostered by liberals and blessed in a remarkably superficial way by a former Supreme Court justice. It has to do with the moral necessity of joining illegal action to legal consequence. One who acts against the law, if he is to act virtuously and responsibly, must always take the consequences; otherwise, his act is necessarily tainted in the eyes of good men.

The principle obviously is of interest to those in power. It is a more or less conscious vindication of the social, political, and indeed religious status quo. It aims with vigor at the maintenance of law and order in whatever sector, in order to bring even the most passionate conscience under control of unchangeable, presumably beneficent, public authority.

If good men and women, acting in bad times on behalf of serious change in the very nature and function of public authority, can be so coerced, it is quite clear that an impassable limit has been established. Ethical men may, in such a way, even become a powerful support to an evil regime. In paying tribute to the courts, the law, the penal system, they become witnesses to the validity of the structures they seek to confront. Jails, law courts, police, and the social arrangements which depend upon their smooth functioning proceed on schedule to isolate and stifle dissent. The last state of things thus becomes worse than the first.

It was presumed two years ago that the Catonsville resisters would play their appointed role faithfully, as indeed for some time we did. We remained in peace after our action, and submitted to arrest. We engaged lawyers, faced the courts, prepared our defense, conscious that the outcome of our case was preordained by rigorous secular gods both Calvinist and Caesarian in nature. In due process "guilty" was the verdict returned against us. The charade of appeals went forward; we were free on bail; free, that is to a point. By court order there could be no public speech that touched on specific areas of illegal, even though nonviolent, action. Indeed, in an excess of zeal which the courts never thought seriously to enforce, I was forbidden to preach—it being thought, in view of my felonious proclivities, that I could only offer an inflammatory gloss on essentially harmless texts.

I am led to reflect, at this point, how the worst social impasses serve only to build up the forces of man's mind and heart for a cataclysmic breakthrough. At least in some cases. In many others, perhaps the majority, a kind of diffusion of energy, a regressive tolerance builds up, compounded of illusion and hopelessness. One lives with cancer even while it grows internally—as long as we can hang on to the small chance that it is not terminal. So with a certain kind of liberal hope—extinguished by the Kennedy downfall, flaring briefly under the words of McCarthy, at length adjusted to Nixon. For such an ethos to make do, not only must Black aspirations suffer "benign neglect" but any movement of the spirit that seriously challenges a rotting social system will be treated to a heavy dosage of like euphemisms.

But we of Catonsville were cursed or blessed; in any case our readings of the time were different, as were our readings of what religion required of us. What are presumably virtuous men to do when, two years after they have staked their lives on the sanity of their fellowmen, insanity still prevails? To some of us, one thing at least seemed clear. We could by no means presume that the crime-trial-punishment sequence must remain intact simply because two years ago it made sense. Something else might be required; the Vietnam War was more violent and widespread than ever; the march of power proceeded with unexampled boldness, straight on toward foreign and domestic disaster. More victims were dying, wider areas were devastated, the nation was caught, shamed, and traumatized, in the trap which itself had fabricated and sprung. More, the hopes of the early peace movement were wasted by attrition and false promises, within and without; the large-scale reinforcements of resisters from student ranks, workers, Blacks, middle class, failed to appear. We of Catonsville were some years older, and as tired as anyone else; yet the next moves were still up to us. Or so it seemed, and seems.

Some of us decided to continue resistance, to refuse jail.

For how long, we do not know. With what effect, we do not know. Whether we can create in the breach a network of responsibility and support which will allow us to move about, to be heard on occasion, to meet the press, to write and publish, remains to be seen. Everything has literally to be created from whole cloth, to be improvised. We shall have to try, at least.

For white Americans like ourselves, an attempt to create an underground presence which will be nonviolent and politically audible is indeed a chancy one. We are neither Black Panthers, Frenchmen opposing Vichy, the German confessing church in the thirties, Algerians under occupation, members of the National Liberation Front. It would be disastrous to apply to our situation the realities of colonialism or occupation; and any analogies between ourselves and the third world, or ourselves and historic minorities in our own country, must be explored with extreme reserve.

At the same time, analogies are not to be despised. Our government is not merely courting disaster in its irresponsible war abroad, it is setting its face more and more firmly against peaceable change as long as that change threatens the status quo. Such a political atmosphere, if pushed far enough, favors the change it so dreads; it bursts the pods of discontent, resistance, and violence, and scatters the seed far and wide. A profound and widespread sense of fraternity is created across time and distance, between disenchanted Americans and the suppressed masses of Asia, Africa, and Latin America. How long can the raw energy of violated, enraged men be stemmed at home, when it draws its vitality from all sides, even from the very forces that seek to suffocate it? No one can say, least of all those who control, for the present, the course of public authority and the exercise of power.

Perhaps in such times one had best place consideration of purely political gain firmly aside. The odds are simply too great against us to be able to measure our actions solely or primarily against such a scale. If this is so, and I think it may be so, another far more mysterious criterion of action must be involved. It is simply the "suffering fidelity" of which Bonhoeffer wrote in Hitler's Germany. One takes the onslaught trusting to the rightness of his course of action, determined upon so simple a thing as being human. Such may, in the long run, be the only useful course for now. Moving anonymously about the country, speaking and meeting with small groups of friends, encouraging an analysis of our lives, our structures, where a breakthrough may be possible; and perhaps above all showing that such a course is practically (and psychologically) possible—in such a way that myth of omnipotence of the "system" is punctured in one small instance. The alternatives are widened, at least, in one case.

To men and women of the third world, the above must seem a minimal program indeed. Could not Americans, skilled as they presumably are in every technical field from the micro world to the stars, also construct fabulous and imaginative methods of resistance? Does not Dewey's famous principle of "transfer of knowledge" come into play here?

The questions by implication fail to take into account several realities. The first has to do with the nature of political resistance, which cannot by any means be equated with technique. Indeed technical competence, exercised in an atmosphere of cold war competitiveness, consumer economics, and progressive militarization, is quickly evacuated of the interest due to truly historical events. We are left with very little—the vulgarizing of human instinct, junkers in political seats of power, distraction as a way of life, raucous appeals to trivialities and luxuries, the consumer cornucopia pouring out its vast retail heap of polluting junk. Most people are swept under by this stream of "goods and services"; they are pressurized and processed and finally anesthetized against moral choice or movement. Even the student resisters, for whom the war has provided an occasion for a profound revulsion against national absurdity, are shaken as to the future; where there is so much to hate, the task of finding something to love is Herculean indeed.

And yet we think this must be a definition of human movement; the task of finding, in the urban dump yard of our civilization, some clue, some sign, of the presence of love; what direction to take, whom to join with, how to release in a celebrational and useful way these spiritual energies at our command.

At our command, and yet not yet. The American psyche cannot become the fraternal instrument of world change until it has undergone its dark night of the soul. I do not mean this statement to be mystifying or abstract. Quite the contrary. I mean something quite simple; Americans have not only been alienated from world spiritual developments by runaway technology; they have been a vast alienating force in most of the Western world. Moreover, in the third world, the vicious circle in which they are caught at home (the engineering of an inhuman future) has widened into a system of military and economic control and repression. Spiritually isolated from the strivings of men everywhere for justice, decency, and the goods of the spirit, America could export only those dark obsessions which go by the most euphemistic and deceptive of phrases: the American way of life.

The breaking of this iron ring will be accomplished only by the shrewdest blows, repeatedly struck, until the weak points at the circle are broken and Americans themselves are free to join the human fraternity.

As I write this, newspapers are filled with the account of the celebration of "Earth Day" in America. The news is to our point; blows struck in midair, accomplishing nothing. While America continues fervently to pollute and destroy the environment of millions of helpless people abroad, and expands her Eastern war into Laos and Cambodia, a nervous call goes forth to "save our country's environment." A more absurd deflection of true purpose could hardly be imagined.

Right thinking! An issue is genuine only when it is organically in relation to every other issue; in this case, to the impact of militarized consumer–technology on the fate of man. But to the vast majority of Americans, discouraged by the inadequate political gestures of the past years, and desperately seeking some ground to stand on, the "Earth Day" was a sunny and simple hour of relief from the cruel winter solstice of their discontent. Any issue is better than none. The war in Vietnam, which was once Kennedy's war, and then Johnson's war, is now Nixon's war. That it has been from the start, and on their own soil, and in their own burned and violated flesh, the war of the Vietnamese peasants, and that bombs and napalm now fall indiscriminately on the flesh of Laotians and Cambodians, is beside the point. A fact too large for ingesting, too hot for political resistance, simply beyond adequate coping.

Ultimately, beyond coping, since it requires too strong a measure of those qualities which can flourish only when a people have become conscious of their own human losses and begin to create the tools of human gain. Simply, we have not lost enough, or suffered enough, or grown conscious. We lack as a consequence community, imagination, fervor, right thinking, compassion, courage, hope, ingenuity. For the present, "in order to be healed, our illness must get worse."

5. A FAMILY LETTER

5/30/70
Sat.

Dear Ones.

Just got the news through friends about Mom. No need to say how troubling this is though I am reassured about her response after operation. And above all by your being there on hand, faithful as always.

Well I can pray and think of you all and hope with all my heart Mom will make it once more. One can so long to be there & of course I do, & wish Phil also were at hand. But then there are the times—deadly as they are—and our job—which we have not so much taken on ourselves as been summoned for. And I try to measure the pain of separation from you all, against the suffering of so many who are not only helpless or unable to cope, but (which I take to be most crushing to the spirit) have had no choice in their own fate, from birth to death.

We all have had that choice: and in the lives of one another, we have the opportunity to choose something richer and wider than just one life. I take that as a great grace.

And am at peace as I pray you are too: knowing that God who weighs the world and finds himself shortchanged, often by believers, still settles for one or two just men. In whose company we can hope with some reason to be found.

Please kiss Mom for me and tell her of my love and prayers; and even presence to her, as Phil's also.

I am thriving to the point of obscenity, obeseness, etc. The public media continue their interest in my project. So beyond doubt does the FBI. Which accounts for the fact that I continue to live like the Son of Man who said he was living like the beasties of the field. When you look at your ravaged greens & think of the little blind fluffs who make it, think of them kindly in my name.

You might say in an inept metaphor the FBI is getting gently chewed out in the night. HA and LUV.

P.S. Jerry's letter just came, great relief. Agree wholeheartedly foolhardiness my appearing there. No, yez will as usual hold the fort; and we'll give the buzzards NO MEAL this time.

6. NOTES FROM THE UNDERGROUND; OR I WAS A FUGITIVE FROM THE FBI

May 7 marks exactly a month since I packed the small red bag I had bought in Hanoi, and set out from Cornell, looking for America. So far, it has been a tougher and longer voyage than the one which set me down in North Vietnam some two years ago.

In the course of that month, I have changed domicile some six times; this in strict accord with a rule of the Jesuit Order, making us, at least in principle, vagabonds on mission; "It is our vocation to travel to any place in the world where the greater glory of God and the need of the neighbor shall impel us." Amen, brothers.

It may be time for a modest stock-taking. The gains sought by such felonious vagrancy as mine are, in the nature of things, modest to the point of imposing silence on the wise. The "nature of things" being defined simply as: power. It is entirely possible that any hour of any day may bring an end to the game; the wrong chance meeting, a thoughtless word of a friend, a phone tip—the possibilities are without end. But one takes this for granted, and goes on, knowing that practically all of us are powerless, that the line dividing the worth of one's work from inertia and discouragement is thin indeed. (What manner of man today exudes confidence, moral spleen, righteousness, sense of messiahship at once cocksure, and dead serious? God, who grants us very little these days, at least keeps us from that.)

But what can I hope to accomplish, on the run as I am, having to improvise and skimp and risk being ridiculous, or plain two-cents wrong? How can I reject honored presumptions of conduct, like "the good man is responsible for his actions"; he "pays up on demand"? Or the older Socratic dictum: "one owes the state restitution for broken law, violated order?"

The method of Martin King, violation of local or state law and submitting to jail, had a great deal going for it; circumstances supported the principle. Being in jail was invariably an appeal to a higher jurisdiction. It brought the attention of national authorities to the fact of local or state violations; it brought pressures from above. Such a tactic, apart from its mystique, was in fact a calculated political act. It dramatized in the face of brutal local forces, purportedly of law and order, the captive state of the virtuous, at the mercy of lesser jurisdictions. And it seemed for a while to pay off. Both Kennedy and Johnson professed to be moved by innocence under fire; they pledged themselves to amelioration, not merely in freeing demonstrators, but in bringing legal redress of widespread wrong.

Alas and alas, how could such a tactic apply to me and my friends? What superior jurisdiction would rush to action on the occasion of our jailing? To whom could we appeal? To the International War Crimes Tribunal? To the United Nations? To the World Court? In our instance, straw men all; the United States has pushed them flat, along with the other superpowers. No, those of us who are willing to go to jail must seek our analogies elsewhere than in the civil rights movement if we would seem to be politically serious (as indeed, Philip, David, John, Tom, and Marjorie are, and will be heard from).

But as far as national due process is concerned, the highest appeal courts duly swept aside the issues we tried to raise. That, of course, did not remove the issues; they grow hotter and more lethal every day. The war is mounting in fury. The Congress, the universities, the churches, bankers, workers, decent citizens of all stripes, separately or in concert, are talking to stone-deaf power. For at least the past six months, when jail was becoming a nearer and larger threat, the students with whom I worked for three years, and for whom my decision seemed to be of some import, said to me time and again, with imploring: "When they come for you, don't go in!"

The festival at Cornell offered a delicious opportunity, too good to let pass. Some 10,000 students had come together for a post-Woodstock festival of arts, politics, communal living, all in honor of nonviolence and Catonsville. Such a gathering, it seemed to me, must not be taken lying down, lost in wondering admiration. According to certain presumptions, mainly of university officials (whose relief was guarded, oblique, but in the air), I was indeed going to jail. But those to whom I was responsible, in the Church and the resistance, had other urgings, rarely expressed, often legible in faces and eyes. Would I be inventive on the night, open to other voices, other directions?

Irresistible. At 7:40 P.M. on Friday, April 17, I ended ten rustic days in hiding on the land, and entered the great Barton Hall, scene of last year's forty-eight-hour live-in after the Black seizure of the Student Union. Scene, too, of ROTC reviews and maneuvers and confrontations; the only place on campus where gun-toting is "invisible" and legal to this day. I was decked out gorgeously, like an outer-space insect, in big goggles, motorcycle helmet and jacket, surrounded by a troupe of students, variously hirsute, hippy, fierce, and celebrational. Waskow was thundering away on stage, the Freedom Seder was in progress. The moment arrived when Elias the prophet is summoned, figure of providence for all those in legal jeopardy. Supposing that I qualified, I walked on stage.

The next hour and a half were stormy indeed. I recall a sense of weightlessness, almost of dislocation; the throng of young faces, singing, dancing, eating, the calls of support and resistance. Much love, many embraces, the usual press of journalists. Then, in a quiet moment, a friend whispered: "Do you want to split?"

It was all I needed. Why not indeed split? Why concede, by hanging around, that the wrong-headed powers owned me? Why play mouse, even sacred mouse, to their cat game? Why turn this scene into yet another sanctuary, so often done before, only delaying the inevitable, the hunters always walking off with their prize?

When the lights lowered for a rock group, I slipped off backstage. Students helped lower around me an enormous puppet of one of the twelve apostles, in use shortly before by a mime group. Inside the burlap, I had only to hold a stick that kept the papier-mâché head aloft, and follow the others, making for a panel truck in which we were to pack the costumes. The puppets were pitched aboard; I climbed in, blind as a bat, sure of my radar, spoiling for fun. It was guerrilla theater, a delight, just short of slapstick. An FBI agent ran for the phone, our license plate was recorded, the chase was on. But our trusty van, hot with destiny, galloped for the woods, and we made it.

The rest is modest history, of sorts. My brother and David Eberhardt were picked up in New York the following Tuesday amid a hue and cry worthy of bigger game. I settled in, here and there, for the short or long haul, resigned to the fate of harmless creatures in the open hunting season of our society; neither hoof nor claw, only protective coloration. A kind of roadrunner, stopping here and there to gain breath and take soundings with friends, and then move on.

The first month has been an interesting experiment: the breaking of idols. That myth of omnicompetence surrounds almost any large federal authority, a myth inflated despite all sorts of contrary available evidence: the successive CIA fiascos in Southeast Asia and elsewhere, the wrong Marines on the wrong beaches, the utter inability (a spiritual failure) to touch the sources of unrest at home. Was there something here to be dramatized? The FBI is quite possibly composed of earnest, stern, honorable Romans. (I am always made to feel secure when meeting them, there are so many Catholics; even when they stoop to conquer, poking under beds for priests, they never forget their folklore; it is always; "Are you there, Father Dan?") FBI training, so the cruder movies tell us (we have little other information available) includes grueling hours spent over hot computers, fingerprint recorders, rifle ranges. The bureau undoubtedly has all the men and money required to track down public enemies like myself. There has not yet been a strike threat by the agents for salary emolument; nor has J. Edgar ever called agonized public attention to rusty six-shooters or empty saddles.

Grant them all that. Still I suggest my case offers interesting evidence of a striking failure of power, beginning with the FBI and extending even to Vietnam. It is a failure of overkill technology, of pacification, of search-and-destroy missions, of Vietnamization, of indiscriminate trampling of national boundaries.

I am prepared even, subject to acts of God, to set down a tentative principle, a kind of metatemporal translation from the sayings of Chairman Jesus; "Where the fish travel in schools, it is useless to work with even the most sophisticated reel. The only solution: metamorphose into a fish." Also to our point, is a warning drawn from strict textual scrutiny of the New Testament. To wit, there is only the barest internal evidence that Luke 5:10 ("Fear not, I shall make you fishers of men") has literal reference to the FBI.

I could go on, but perhaps a point is made. A dizzying thought occurs to me, shaking my hand as I write. Could it be that your humble servant, without script or staff, might be an instrument for demythologizing Big Bro Justice? I like the idea, even as a voice reminds me it is fraught with presumption.

But in face of all that power, all that legitimacy, all those hunters and hounds—what can I count on when the chips are down?

Mr. Mitchell, it is reported, was recently presented with a shiny night stick by a local police department. It was inscribed: "To the top cop." He carried it home under his arm, grim with satisfaction. Now the head of the Justice Department has at his disposal, directly or through others, some hundreds of thousands of night sticks and assorted other hardware, goods and services, plus the hands itching to wield them on command. I contemplate all this vast panoply of power; and I am not shaken, any more than Buddha under his plane tree. For I have other armaments, resources, and visions, of which Mr. Mitchell can know little. My friends, in the main. I number among them, for a start, professors, resisters, priests and nuns, some Black Panthers, a deceased corpulent Pope (pregnant with a new world), many men and women at present serving time, Kurt Vonnegut, David Smith and his sculpture, Corita, my mother of eighty-five years (a woman of rare fiber and beauty), John of the Cross and his road map for a dark night, Paul Goodman (crotchety and visionary), the Vietnamese. I could go on, Mr. Mitchell, but you get the idea. From the swamps of Asia, from the American underground and jails and campuses a word goes forth: "When the chips are down," the little people ask "who are your friends?" And further: "Who owns this land anyway?"

The question burns like a night flare. The night sticks come running. But the night sticks can do nothing; they do not signify. In the deepest sense (forever lost to top cops) they are ersatz; wooden limbs in place of living ones. They substitute woodenly and hardly at all, for lost friendship, lost communion, contemplatives and activists, for friends and countrymen and dreamers, open minds, closed mouths, the network of men and women who at need can be counted on to "harbor, aid and abet," and, as the saying goes, generally mother up the works and agents of power.

My being at large is thus related, in some quirky way I leave to others, to an infinitely more striking historical occurrence. That happening is evident by now to everyone in the world, except the President of the U.S.A., his cabinet and chiefs of staff, J. Edgar and his sleuths, the CIA, the Daughters of the American Revolution, and General Westmoreland. (The ultimate person named, recently addressed the penultimate ladies, in the following words: "Our own revolution has ended the need for revolution forever." Yes, perhaps.) The occurrence I refer to should nonetheless be stated, for benefit of us all. Simply, Vietnam cannot be defeated. I take the fact to heart, an article of human faith, constantly buttressed by news out of Asia and Washington. In public places and private, I cherish it, and smile and smile to myself, the delight of a man to whom sanity is surprise, gift, delight. Translated to my life and hard times, the fact means something; if our friends and I use our wits, our act is going to have a long, long run, on Broadway and beyond.

It's because we own the land. The night sticks of the chief cop are no apt substitute, given the real world, for organs, limbs, compassion, brain, historical sense, patience, courage, the nonviolent resources of good friends. The top cop, even as he invents more electronic junk, censors, intercoms, copters, taps, bugs, computers, *et al.*, becomes less and less able to be human: spontaneous, free-spirited, humorous, spunky—liturgical. I think we can match him, by being some of these things, at least some of the time. I think as a result we can liberate even top cops, causing them to commit what one ex-agent assured me was the most heinous of internal crimes: embarrassing the Bureau.

Finally, if they do run me down, I will claim a win anyway. I will go off to jail in better spirits than my captors.

But in any case, we own the land. You cannot (by analogy) make a bomber pilot or a military adviser or a search-and-destroy mission, or, God help us, an ignorant American private into a guerrilla—for theater, for war or peace. None of these, nor the sum of their might, nor the full discharge of their ferocity, can claim to own the land. No one of them was born there, no one of them loves it there or has roots there. You cannot airlift or import or graft on a substitute for the fact of birth, the genetic mystery of a love that is stronger than death. You cannot buy the people, their support, their trust. All who invade and murder and lay waste the land can only perform such "operations" as we read of daily—ending where such mad surgery always ends—in extermination.

A clue for Americans. There are some of us who claim to own this land. We do not hold current lien or title or mortgage, or want to. We have no political power. Our claim is based finally on the strength of our intuitions—on a sense of history generally lost sight of, despised, or suppressed. To wit: man has an inalienable right, in Kent State as in Song My, in resister's jail or resister's underground, to life, liberty, and the pursuit of happiness.

That "pursuit" is indeed something more than an honorable dead letter. Pursuit: a metaphor that draws blood—a chase, a hunt, an FBI-wanted list, jeopardy, dislocation, the poverty of man on the move. Those who pursue happiness must endure unhappiness, the dark night of resistance, doubt, delusion, nightmare; because they pursue decency and a human future, for the despised and expendable, the wretched of the earth.

The first month is over, the future is charged with surprise. Come, Holy Spirit.

7. TWICE-BORN MEN: THE UNMASKING OF FEAR

Murray Kempton calls the New York Panthers in court "twice-born men." And he is right. Those men are so in command of their lives, after emerging from a year's residence in the New York "Dispos-All" jail mechanism (designed to reduce the most fractious spirits to near hamburger), as to astonish any human eye privileged to rest on them. Astonishment, delight. I take them as a sign, in the rigorous sense of that word. A sign of the unkillable resources of the spirit, reasserting a new season for mankind, surrounded as we are by the wintriness of spirit that assails and freezes the heart's core.

Spring has come, despite all. To say that the human signs of the event are unexpected and austere is another way of paying tribute to the variety and surprise of nature itself, of man himself. Which is to say, and to share with you, the entire normalcy of signs like Panthers in court, my brother Philip in jail, myself on the run, the jeopardy cheerfully shouldered by friends, the flowers and trees and streams of the landscape; the whole schtick, one might say.

I have to imagine as I write: all of you, your reactions to the last weeks, what the swift pace of things might mean and not mean to you. Discomfort, I imagine in many cases, exhilaration in others. And always, your reaction to jailbirds, their migrations and cagings, reactions tempered by the fiery events of deaths, invasions, duplicity in high places, the deaf muteness of churches, the clash of armies by day and night—that monstrous normalized sound of modern man's chief activity—something like the pneumatic drills on New York streets, outrageous but inevitable.

Do jailbirds lose their singing voices? We are trying not to, from Aldersen, Lewisburg, Allenwood, and all the other great aviaries where the species are caged and studied under optimal conditions—with an ironic view to their survival—and even their multiplication. Ecologically speaking, it would be hopeful to view the prisons as a vast network of living laboratories: all the guards, probation officials, wardens, and subalterns as more or less skilled technologists in aiding the testing and deepening our spirit. Also courts, judges, public prosecutors, et al., unwittingly segregating certain ideal, exotic, spontaneous spirits; so that, finally, man himself may survive; so that Newspeak and Doublethink and Gobbledygook and Preventive Strike and Military Incursion and Benign Neglect, those murky possessive spirits, may be dispossessed of their prey. . . .

Well, one can dream.

One of the features of a month like the one just past strikes my attention. It concerns the shuffling of relationships, a new place introduced by new sorts of action. People who finally come to accept Catonsville find their fingertips tingling with a new onset of—what? Fear, dread, the unknown? Something like this. Too much is pushed at them, too fast. They can easily accept the fact that one is bound for jail, or is already jailed: it is as normal, say, as war itself. A gun goes off in the night, a new border is crossed; we have seen all this before; it is enraging, irresponsible, horrifying. But after all, one did respond: one was in D.C. at considerable inconvenience for the latest massing of colors. And meantime, there are children at home, there is a job to attend to, there is normalcy calling for reassertion. Which is to say, very deep in one's mind: enough is enough, even of a good thing.

In my case, this is just the rub. I am too much of a good thing in the minds of some I have encountered in the past weeks. Admirable men no doubt; but to offer succor or harbor or one's pulpit, one's home or hospitality? That is another kettle of fish entirely, and it smells not good.

It may be of some value to reflect on such reactions. I am struck, first of all, by the fear that wells up in many when I put in an appearance. All to the good. We are all fearful in somewhat the sense that we cast a shadow as we walk. It is natural to us; fear reminds us of the dark side of our soul, the depths of ignorance or self-deception or obscurity that dog us.

I remember with what insight Phil took up the persistence of fear at one of our last public gatherings together. He began, not with accusation or moralism or a diagnosis of "them." But with ourselves, him and me. How we had been fearful men, from childhood, from schooling, from obedience, from almost very formative pressure of our past. How we had had to work vith our fear, facing it, being compassionate with it, knowing hat "it" was not some demon to be cast out once and for all, ut a coloration of the spirit, a filter experience, both chastening nd teaching us, keeping the ego within bounds, slowing us to the uman pace of things.

So we fear, commonly, and must learn to live with our ear, even as we are humiliated and brought down to size by t; its sudden welling up, its unexpected assault on energies and ingleness of mind. In a sense, I take even a kind of ironic omfort from the evidence of fear that arises in some at the int of my presence. (Something like the oncoming of death ven! or as though I were peddling albatrosses, to be hung round the neck as peace symbols.) That is to say, I think the wakening of fear on the occasion of a new crisis is also a kind of nmasking of fear. Through their fears, we even come to know ne another better; our quality, our courage and staying power. 3ut perhaps even better, when fear arises in their gorge, men women come to know themselves better.

Sometimes, too, it seems to me that feelings of fear say something ther than danger to one's survival, well-being, security, life as sual. There is another side to this old coin. I mean that I have een able to read, in a moment of dread, the mysterious face of he future, coming very near, summoning me. Do we dread only he noxious, the threatening, the harmful? This, they say, is true f beasts, a kind of conscious radar glimmering away in the dark, n antenna of survival. For us, I think, something else. I do not hink it can be said of us that our fear has only a primitive unction. I think we fear being "twice born." I think we fear he nearing presence of freedom, the face it wears, the smell it xudes, the eye it casts on us. I think we fear the future, in the alpable, embodied sense which life offers us—the suffering of ur brothers, the iron march (in our direction too) of the xterminator's heel.

This is not meant to turn into a dosage of Greeley's Therapy. The question of "getting rid of" our fears is about as futile s the question of getting rid of one's shadow. There is of course ne way. One can choose to walk in the darkness. But if (in

St. John's magnificent metaphor) one walks in the light, then his works, including his fearful works, will be manifest.

I have been earning my keep this month reading, writing, meeting people under various circumstances (note please the anti-Sherlockholmesian vagueness; among fauna of my species this is known as protective coloration). I have been making tapes to substitute for nonappearance, where circumstances made this advisable (above note, again). I have also received the most delightful and heartening subterranean vibrations from friends, evidence of various encouraging goings, comings, communings, co-habitings, eatings and drinkings. The maples on this street meantime (it could be any street, dear FBI) have gone peerlessly about their own business, which given the times, seems mysteriously like my own. Their survival through a cruel and protracted winter can no longer be called conjectural. They have put forth leaves. . . .

Most people, I judge, are simply appalled by the course of recent events, from Kent through Cambodia and the South. I do not wish to be cynical, but I think the Black reaction to the death of whites has about it a certain icy rightness. That is to say, with most of us, today's appall is tomorrow's cold omelet. Systems adjust, including human ones. Simply determining to survive exacts a great human toll; including, no doubt, the protection of one's tolerance toward the omnipresence, the near omnicompetence, of death. That austere smooth gentleman is extending his services, in the good old American way; he now offers a very nearly complete package deal, from the delivery room to Dignified Final Arrangements. The extent of his holdings remains a matter of some surprise, and even raises questions in the Congress. Shortly, however, he will be part of the economic landscape, a Goods and Services Expert to be called on like a milkman or plumber. We will scarcely be able to imagine, after a time, how we ever managed without him.

How in truth do we manage without him? One had best raise the question, while the question has some urgency. Today's untruth is tomorrow's gospel, today's military outrage is tomorrow's cliché, today's Presidential lies are tomorrow's diplomatic move. It is not, I judge, that people do not react in human fashion to such crimes, indeed they often over-react. But their reactions are quickly consumed in the hearth of "normal living." After a while, warming their hands at that fire, they catch themselves wondering why, yesterday (last month, last year) things were better. Or even: yesterday, last year, I was an entirely different person. I am dulled before the fact of death; not by its absence, but by its omnipresence.

One would think a useful reaction to recent weeks would be the serious questioning of how things have gotten so out of hand; what it is in our style, our structures, our families, our professional lives, the ethos, the material needs, the ambitions, the fears (once more) that allow such things to proceed without serious challenge.

I am trying clumsily to say: even the most acute moral sense, operating in a void, is simply useless. Indignation, anger, outrage are useful when they become the cool and tempered tools of social change. When they do, crime may even beget virtue, instead of whimpering or moral indolence or paralysis. But when emotional response drifts about, unanchored to purpose and courage, free-floating and self-indulgent, I am not at all sure that "virtue" does not beget more crime.

Several general trends, I would judge, can now be discerned in American life. (1) The military are in command of events. (Cleaver said recently, he expects a military coup in the U.S. in '72.) I suggest the last thing the military needs is a military coup. They already control the country's foreign policy, in its larger outlines. (2) The solution introduced to any friction point in the world, from Harlem to Cambodia, will therefore inevitably be military, in method and in principle. (3) This situation is likely to endure, with various applications of hot and cold, compromise and outrage, during whatever future we are likely to see. (4) The question arises: how do we make the "peace movement" into a normal, functional way of conducting our human business, if only in limited sectors and among a minority? So that the omnicompetence of the society, as well as its endless power of sucking in almost every new tactic, is reduced. (We are in the time of the slow reduction of the encroaching state; slow, and reduction; not fast, not revolution. The latter is hogwash.) The peace movement is grievously limited by the capacity, money, manpower, technology available to those in the military and in government. This is no news; everyone is hyper-aware of it; I almost said, everyone uses it for his favorite immobilizing excuse. A far more severe limitation on us is our inability to take peacemaking as the form of our lives, the function of our losses and gains, the only and main and "normal" occupation we will ever know. The latest charades in D.C. and at local draft boards is a case in point. Everyone, including the police, did their thing on schedule. Everyone went home to spouse and supper. The war went on. There seemed to be little sense that unless the cities are inundated by people who won't go home, who miss their supper, who are jailed and replaced by other people, a kind of plague of locusts against Egypt, nothing will happen.

The sending of a prayerful petition to the President by several religious leaders was another case in point. Such heated invocations of God, decency, morality are cool indeed by the time our leader's hand rests on them, if indeed it ever does. More painfully, such tactics, at this point, renege on the real question: is not political activity tied to the degree of normalcy, security, routine we are able to dispense with, in the name of some real, visible, vital political changes? Suppose, for instance, each of those religious people, cleric and lay, who had signed the prayer to the President had announced instead that they were not leaving the environs of the White House until some sign was issued from within of a change in war policy. Suppose they were in effect, with their friends, to declare the President a "prisoner of war" in his own citadel. Suppose their students, seminarians, etc., including families, had been urged to come and join—and stay; it being announced that classes would continue, only on that park lawn outside the seat of power.

The peace movement, I suggest, need not look high or wide for its chief weakness. It is ourselves. Neither need Nixon lose sleep reckoning his legions against ours. He sleeps, by all reports, soundly indeed, secure in our weakness, our fear and trembling, our dread of reading the price tag attached to justice, peace, vindication of the powerless; to life itself.

This is already over-long. Let me end here, send to you all my thought of you, my love. The times are wrong. We must break the clocks, for the times belong to us.

8. LIFE AT THE EDGE

Dear Friends:

What follows is a brief and somewhat disjointed attempt to send greetings and best wishes from just under the crust of the planet. There, I can now witness, most good things have their beginning—streams, flowers, springs, sources, and roots, whether of friendship, spirit, or the stillness that both energizes and embraces movement. Given what—judging by such reverberations of wing and hoof as reach me down under—is the general state of heads and hearts in men and beasts almost all over, I am, like God, alive and reasonably well.

Philip, David, and the others are at present rocking in the everlasting arms of mother state. That fact lends urgency to our days and nights and saves us from whimsicality and frivolity—as well as from the creeping paralysis of despair. What can we do, in the way of being their other tongue, their further arm, their vocal thought, the public beat of those strong and most virile hearts? And what is the meaning of this existence that I have undertaken almost by happenstance, in the access of resolve induced by the arrogance of a command: Now come out, you, and prove your virtue by submitting before US! It seems to me I can discover that meaning only in the very act of being here, taking readings and opinions, hearing from friends. But a few reflections occur.

I

(1) Is the idea of a stubborn underground presence itself viable? Something other, I mean, than the underground of the AWOLs? Does it have, can it have, a value which is both symbolic and real—i.e., a sign of hope, a widening of the moral area of resistance? What does it mean to all kinds of people whose communal mood now is deep frustration over the impasse created by rotten (but most calculated) policy?

(2) Presupposing that the answer to the above is "Yes," what

do we do? It seems to me, from very short experience, that across the land there are all sorts of energy nodes smoldering in the gloom, waiting to be turned on full force. Not merely inventiveness in helping one survive, but new ways of creating community, of communicating, of helping people walk out of old shells and strip off old armor.

(3) I can't stress deeply enough the essential modesty of mind that should be its moral accompaniment. We are not Panthers running for cover in the open hunting season of our society. No one of us is going to be allowed, by the hunting-club rules, to lay down his life; there are no bounties on us. At the same time, the natural climate of any surreptitious long-term movement, shifts between paranoia, obsession, and grandiose rhetoric. People waver between yielding to moods of persecution and sounding pronunciamentos about changing the world. However, nothing like this or that is occurring; we are just not that interesting to the big hungry printing machine tumbling its consuming way into tomorrow. Something modest, therefore, in intent and style. (The last account of the "resisting priest" was printed somewhere among the bra ads on page 2,358 of the heavyweight Sunday *Times*. Thus far public interest in my fate.) But all this, I think, is not to the point. Such a criterion as "making it big in the press" violates the long-hauling patience that produces true history. It is important that thousands of people do as many thousands of interesting things, conformed to the measure of their lives, to where they live, with whom they live. Genuine actions always converge—at length. The length—of time, of distance—necessary for such acts to converge depends often (like the movement of glaciers toward a common transformation of landscape) on the submission of each to the historical forces that push from beneath. What takes longest may well be most significant; reverence for needful distance involves something more than an aesthetic.

II

(4) We have to develop new modes of operating, based on new realities before us, the underground, the imprisoned. Both can be "at large" in a new way. Both have to confront the rules of the game which society has developed to keep men under

the lock and key that commonly go by the name "law 'n' order"; i.e., "at small," diminished. (He's pure America, the prisoner or fugitive are only his images, up close.) Anyway, for the present, Phil and I (and others) have the unimaginably exciting chance to explore, from the other side of the mirror, those constricting images that waver about the edge of the imagination, terrorizing, policing, clubbing, shadowing, exacting submission, diminishing man in his best parts and thereby creating the race of inventive dwarfs that, from university, church, home, club, domestic bliss, professional status, march from here to Saigon, to keep the game going. Is it possible to march in a different direction, to a different drummer? One can choose to walk away from his images, as well as toward them. . . .

(5) What we choose is a very old choice. Its expression has varied according to cultures, and I would venture that in the West and East it has never been absent for long. The wandering clerk, the enclosed contemplative. Thomas Merton used to be very strong on these. He had no hesitation in stressing their often illegal character; the "gyrovagues" especially had a strong flair for the outrageous, were often in trouble. Merton used to say that the monk is a man at the edge of both church and society, barely tolerated by either; but being at the edge he has the inestimable advantage of being able to talk with those whose lives are a long pilgrimage at the edge, coming in, going out, pausing here, hoping there, despairing almost always. That edge where the future is both endangered and engendered. Bonhoeffer spoke of this too, his biographer said. Once he realized that he must live at the edge, he was a dead man in both church and state, and knew it.

(6) It is diverting, consoling, pacifying, heart-warming, what have you, to be able to grab a historical analogy that really hits nails on nailheads. The trouble is, once he has nailed down a useful thing, one's natural tendency is to sit on it—mine! Whereas, the real job is to run with it—movement, gift! Could it be that ours is a new form of the perennial hot news, good news, coming on the hot wire? I can only hope so. People are in much more dangerous despair today than, say, a year ago. The interstices of the soul are starting to sizzle and leak; that outward conformity to the bad orders of bad power is cracking their plates. Too many pressures

on the integrity of being! We are not yet South Africa or Germany in the Thirties. Still, if all the lamps went out and a kind of ultraviolet could light up the real men in our midst, it would show a pretty empty landscape. Can we bring good news? Can we—invisible in principle and under jeopardy, paying for crimes or postponing payment—can we be visible to our brothers and sisters? One can only hope.

III

(7) Shortly before the cops came to the door, I was going out the back window, figuratively speaking. Now definitely that was not a good (read: American) scene. One cannot entirely dismiss the objections of those who would have me, their good virtuous man, their ikon in fact, going to the door, white of face but firm of chin, pulse quickening with moral resolve, wrists offered to the handcuffs, riding off into the sunset, all stops off on Handel's *Messiah*. (Obviously, I don't mean to caricature those of my brothers and sisters who chose to go. But I can poke fun, and do, at those who concluded: of course he will do such and such; and so, before the fact, already had me in prison, in more ways than one.) Anyway, we have here an instance of what I might call J. Edgar's Law for the Unconfessing Churches. That law, in the past two years, was reviewed by command of our Peerless Leader, and now includes a post-Catonsville Codicil. Formerly, this law had to do with the Neat Arrangement arrived at, like a good morganatic marriage (it was one), by mutual consent and respect for territorial imperatives. Some few First Estate clerics even got to the White House for Sunday A.M. brunch, in the course of which, it is said, a humorous and harmless charade was sometimes played: one party trying on the biretta of the other, the other marching up and down briefly in the gleaming shako of the White House guard. Some read ominous things into such scenes; others, more hardened souls, took it in stride—the symbol after the fact, they said.

Anyway, some clerics made a mess of the arrangement. Some few. Then the law was amended: *Clerics, though in their ranks may be found some few deviants, are still gentlemen. Because they are clerics. Therefore, having written a check, they will pay up on demand. Because checks are for cashing. Obviously.*

The intent of the amended law was at least twofold. First it aimed to separate clerics in the public eye (and in a bad time) from Mississippi boat gamblers, Times Square drifters, touts from all over, car thieves, pimps, unsavory characters generally. Because, of course, ours had been a Moral Witness—two years after Catonsville that was evident to any blind man. Then, second, it was to the advantage of those who call the shots for all of us (it being part of their knowledge and our ignorance that some citizens should live and some die) that we have the good grace to follow through on the game which we, after all, had initiated. (Had there meantime been a kind of run-around-end play, the goal line sown thick with FBI men dressed like tackles and guards?) In any case, it is the function of a superior wisdom, based on superior access to knowledge (more facts, in fact), that better men than we—men elected to high office by the majority of citizens—at a mutually agreed time and place lock us up.

The moral of all this (purely partisan, admittedly): you can fool some of the clerics nearly all of the time, but, etc., etc.

IV

I will close this installment with one observation, which I leave it to friends to work over. Simply this: The time will shortly be upon us, if it is not already here, when the pursuit of contemplation becomes a strictly subversive activity. This is the deepest and at the same time, I think, the most sensible way of expressing the trouble into which my brother and I have fallen. What else have we been up to these several years? We have been trying mightily to avoid the distraction from reality which is almost a stigma of the modern mind. We have been practicing, with very mixed success, so simple a thing as concentration; we have been sticking with the pertinacity of bloodhounds to the trail—to the blood of Christ, another name for history in process, in movement.

We have been trying to remember man; to re-member him, in the rigorous liturgical sense—to exercise anamnesis, the heart of the eucharistic command and privilege: when you do this, remember me. Which is to say, stay with history, make something of it, by falling within its main lines of action, the breaking of bread, the sharing of wine; make a community whose life will also be available to history.

We have been trying not to forget, not to forget either by way of amnesia or distraction. We have had very little time or patience for celebrations which we took to be merely another form of induced forgetfulness. We could not celebrate something which we were perhaps refusing to let happen—which might possibly be our own death; or short of that, the will to embrace, in however fragmented a way, the insecurity and loss we were being called to.

I am quite sure of what I mean, however badly it comes out. I am convinced that contemplation, including the common worship of the believing, is a political act of the highest value, implying the riskiest of consequences to those taking part. Union with the Father leads us, in a sense charged with legal jeopardy, to resistance against false, corrupting, coercive, imperialist policy. We have been living a recorded history long enough for the evidence now to be in. The saints were right: their best moments were on the run, in jail, at the edge of social acceptability. Tactics, modes of response, vocabulary, the public uses (and misuses) of mysticism—all were entirely secondary. They might win or not in the short run. They might or might not succeed—in Bonhoeffer's phrase—in putting a stick in the wheel of power; they would try for that modest disruption. But the heart of the matter lay elsewhere. It lay in the irreducible content of a memory that could not finally suffer brainwashing; some event to "remember" (and therefore to reproduce—an image, an action captive to choice), some reality to call into unity and peace, to bind up and heal our broken estate.

We are back with our image of life at the edge. That edge turns against the one who chooses to live and die without weapons. His freedom has made it possible for him to choose another way of life than the death of his brother. But this does not mean—when pseudo-history moves up close with its massed demands on body and soul—that a man will not suffer death himself. Quite the contrary. Have you ever heard of death by solitude, by ostracism? Of the "extramural" activities of Christ? (He was born, says the author of the Letter to the Hebrews, outside the walls, *extra muros*, to die; extradited, we would say—a man without a people, cut off from the privileges of community and citizenship.)

Deep waters indeed—to this point, in a time of distemper and alienation. One startling sign of the rightness of a course of action may be the initial sharp outcry against it, in church and state alike.

We ask our friends to go slow in judging us, in turning us out of their minds or rejecting us from their prayers.

9. HOW TO MAKE A DIFFERENCE

It is quite possible (no news at all by now) that my brother Philip and David Eberhardt are in the "hole" at Lewisburg Federal Prison; as nearly as we can learn, they were consigned there on or about July 8. For those unfamiliar with penal arrangements, it may be useful to describe "the hole," whose existence is not widely discussed in prison guide books. Every prison boasts, in one or another form, such a facility: a small isolated cell, with or without mattress and toilet, in which the condign crime of punishment may go forward for indefinite periods. No outside exercise, visitors, contacts, books; often, in winter, no heat (or excess heat, no ventilation); even, in extreme cases, no clothing. Such is the common threat; such often the fate assigned those who prove, in some way or other, recalcitrant against (the words are Philip's) "rehabilitation experts, under whose care one is transformed into a robot or a drone."

Philip is declining to be so transformed. His decision may be of some moment, for the church also. As he was the first priest in our national history to become a political prisoner, so now his presence in the hole changes that dungeon literally into a "priest hole"—a throwback (throw forward?); in any case a historic link with other periods and other priests. In Elizabethan England, one remembers, Jesuits and others at the mercy of public justice often hid out in airless pockets for days on end, while pursuivants sacked the premises in search of them.

But now that these men are holed in, it seems necessary to change our language in regard to their situation, as well as that of Bobby Seale and other "political prisoners." I am suggesting that it is no longer accurate to speak of such men in these terms. Rather, they must be thought of as hostages of war.

A few facts. Philip and David have been kept for some three months, in a high-security prison, against all precedent—which invariably consigns political prisoners to low-security work camps. They have been warned, moreover, that there will be no change in their prison conditions until I have surrendered or been captured. Moreover, some time before the date when we were to surrender for our Catonsville "crime," we were told that once we were behind bars the judge would hold hearings leading to reduction of sentence. Those hearings have since been held in regard to Tom Lewis, and his sentence of six years cut by half; he had surrendered on the appointed day. But Philip's sentence stands unchanged, because for some ten days he refused induction into the armed forces of federal justice.

In simple mathematics, Philip is thus paying with three years of his life for ten days at large—a ration of one hundred days in prison for each day he resisted. This, I submit, is a ratio of punishment to crime which recalls the Nazi or Fascist treatment of hostages of the Maquis, the South African or Angolan disposition of captured guerrillas, the Ky bullies moving against Buddhists and students, the United States incarceration of Panthers without bail. The war has indeed come home, and Bobby Seale, David, and Philip are among the first to be captured behind the lines.

Prior to the latest crisis at Lewisburg, a pattern of repressive treatment was slowly heating up the atmosphere. The facts are known to us by now. Philip was placed under suspicion of organizing a penal strike, his cell was repeatedly shaken down and his personal writing seized, his mail was overcensored, seized, sent back to friends (even to formerly approved correspondents), and used to attempt to trace my whereabouts. A memorandum was issued to guards to watch him as a potentially dangerous organizer. He was subject to shakedown search of person, in the yard; for what, we are in the dark. He and Eberhardt were singled out for two minor violations, even though they stood in a crowd of prisoners violating the same rule; none of the others was so charged. Finally, the chapel vestry where Philip had vested for Mass was ransacked: for dynamite, firearms, writings—we have no clue.

Much of the foregoing could be called ludicrous; but there are other overtones to the hunt, some of them sobering in the utmost. In May the FBI came for George Mische in Chicago; he is another Catonsville member, for a while underground. The pursuers showed up with guns drawn. On June 27 some one hundred agents, supported by the usual technological fleet, junk, talkies, censors, and God knows what else, invaded the wedding of two friends in Baltimore in pursuit of your correspondent. There was no sacred space that day; church, sanctuary, reception room, basements, closets, all received the search-and-destroy treatment. At one particularly frightening moment, when a balloon happened to pop, guns jumped from agents' hips. Which is to say, priesthood and nonviolent ethos and nonviolent friends aside, what the agents expect is exactly the skills they are used to, trained to. Violence they can deal with, by more of same. It is nonviolence that stops them short. I was not at the wedding.

But anyone who would presume, in face of the foregoing, that the FBI is only mildly interested in my capture is surely ignoring some serious facts. The reason for their continuing interest is not hard to come upon. There is in fact a surge of public sympathy for such an attempt as mine to counter the war, to counter the death game, to resist the growing repression of peacemakers. People are interested, not only in the fate of prisoners, but in alternatives to prison. The case of the first priest who stayed out in the cold, who avowed neither to take up arms nor to flee the country, to govern his life by a calculated personal risk, talking and appearing in public on occasion, thereby facing a longer prison sentence at the end: this is a formula which both awakens public response and hottens up the chase.

The day after the Baltimore wedding, a lengthy interview with me appeared in *The New York Times*. Two weeks before, I had filmed a half-hour interview with NBC; I have also met with small groups of local people in many cities, with AWOL's, resisters, ministers and priests, students, professors.

Inevitably, larger questions have come up. I sense, apart from all questions of my survival or fate, a personal and public malaise, running deep and hard. More people than we readily imagine have reached a stalemate of such proportions as chill the joy and assail the integrity of marriage, work, religion, education of children, the direction and meaning of life itself. Liberal hopes for electoral solutions are largely dashed by the deaths of the saviors. There is a growing realization that, even if the iron cope lowered on the nation by the Nixon engineers is raised, no liberal program, whether of a President Lindsay or Brewster or Burns or Drinan or Gardiner, could long survive the fury of the right; policies of decent deformism, redress of injustice, a more modest role for the military, a less lethal national presence in the world—events since the Chicago convention have passed such men by.

No, we must dig deeper into self-understanding and societal understanding, before solutions worthy of serious scrutiny appear. Which is simply to say, we must lose more, suffer more, experiment more, risk more, trust one another more. The crisis is of such enormous extent and depth that all solutions based on the sanity and health and recoverability of current structures are quickly proven wrong, untimely, unmanageable, bureaucratically infected; the same old kettle of fish, stinking worse than ever in the boiling juices of change.

And this is where a few of us are trying, as best we may, to come in. From the underground, from prison, the movement might have some light cast on it. I make this statement in the full realization of what it implies; up to the present there has been very little that could be called a serious movement at all. There have been moves toward mitigation, moral gestures, protests, civil dissent, sporadic counter-violence. There is a great deal of cultural unrest among youth, controlled readily by the carnivorous national culture, which eats children alive. There have been spasmodic excursions to D.C., drawing enormous migrations of people from their home cotes. But all such happenings have not issued in much; people have undertaken them as moral "extras," always with an eye to the great return: back to job, family, business as usual.

I hope I do not appear with such reflections to be putting down the acts and passion of good people. I want only to get at the obscure truth of things. Where are our lives today? Where are we going? How to make a difference? Even good people are quite generally resigned to endure a great worsening and rotting of the public fabric, as long as such calamity does not strip them naked. How to respond, how to start anew? We are commonly determined neither to go naked (no one willingly dismantles his empire) nor to patch up the old garment (reformism is finished, in politics or tailoring). But what might it mean to weave the fabric of life into a new garment, of such cunning and beauty that the wearer himself is transformed by putting it on—from beggar, outcast, bankrupt, alien, loser, prevaricator, imperialist, racist, exploiter—into a new man? What if in new garments, a new creation were to be born?

"There are mountains of suffering yet to be borne," Gandhi wrote at the time of the great Salt March. "What counts for the future is something as simple as suffering fidelity," Bonhoeffer wrote from prison.

I face the fate of my brother and his friends with a certain tranquillity of spirit. Philip and I have never been able simply to stand about wringing our hands at the latest outrage of Nixon or Johnson or their myrmidons. We have chosen our fate; we have not been condemned to it. Therefore, in face of the latest Lewisburg outrage, it appears that our task is not crushed; it is simply unfinished.

What task? We are summoned to act in unison with our friends, to join in conspiracy, in jeopardy, in illegal nonviolent actions, to hotten up the scene, wherever we are. Such steps will undoubtedly bring more and more revenge upon some of us; whether in the form of longer prison sentences, harassment of our families, solitary confinement in prison, a hotter chase by the FBI. But none of these is to the point, as Philip and I long ago agreed.

What we seek, acting coolly, politically, out of the truth of our lives and tradition, is to pull the mask of legitimacy from the inhuman and blind face of power. We seek at the same time to open the eyes of more and more of our friends, to bring a larger community of resistance into being. We seek moreover to awaken to the facts of life those Americans who continue to grasp at the straws of this or that political promise; and so put off, day after day, year after year, the saving act of resistance, allow the innocent to be imprisoned, the guiltless to be kicked out of America, the good to die.

But if even a few say no, courageously, constantly, clear-sightedly, more will be drawn to say no; fewer likewise will continue to say yes, and so to lose their humanity, their soul, their brothers.

Which is to say, some must be stripped naked. Not as an act of egoism, a side show, but as a skeletal illustration of the state and condition of man today. Some must willingly dismantle their empires.

I think today of Philip, the *alma domus* of the universe in which he took such pleasure, even exaltation. He loves music, food and drink, friends, the game of life, with its checks and counterplays. He has been an inventor of almost every new tool the church has come on in the past decade for her inner renewal, whether of liturgy, social awakening, forms of community. He spoke up early (for a white man) on racism, met the mounting war with all his might. When I think of him, it is of one infected with *joie de vivre;* he is an incurable carrier of that all but vanquished unease, dis-ease, ease. For years he has traveled among people like a Ulysses, voyaging beyond known landmarks, putting in among strangers, marveling at the variety, beauty, terror of the world, the known and unknown; often near shipwreck, near death, but always and everywhere charting new terrain, bringing others to awakening, to debate, to change of heart.

He loved the world well enough to hear the urgent summons to renunciation, to such discipline of emotions as would make him useful as the times worsened. He was willing to test the proposition that celibacy can be as intense an experience of love as sexual relationship, that the *unum necessarium* commended by Christ could also include the *orbs terrarum,* the cape of good hope, Scylla and Charybdis, the love of all people and all things.

In the words of Simone Weil, he put on the universe for garment; for body. Now he is stripped of that garment. He sits or paces in Lewisburg hole, that subterranean box in which society buries, as in its own disordered subconscious, the sweating victims, the untidy raucous voices that above ground or at large would shout the truth too loud. Is he disposed of, like the dead; or is he only buried more deeply in the veins of his people's existence? Knowing him, I would suggest the latter is nearer the truth.

But what of us? How shall we lead our lives? Everything from Vietnam to Lewisburg suggests to me that those who hope at this point for other directions than further repression, further wars, more jailings of resisters, are whistling into the prevailing winds. To expect the worst, to prepare our souls, prophetic or cowardly, for the worst, is the only realism worth talking about. For we are going, downhill and pell-mell, into a dark age, a progress led by Neanderthals armed to the teeth. What lends a sinister despair to their flight plan is the simple knowledge that they face, as do all who misuse the world, simple extinction. The subhumans are struggling against death, the humans are struggling toward birth. Our lifetime sees the conflict joined. We must expect bloodshed, agony, prison, exile, psychic and physical injury, separation, the rupture of relationships, the underground; these are the symptoms and circumstances that precede a new age, a new mankind.

10. FATHER BERRIGAN SPEAKS TO THE ACTORS FROM UNDERGROUND

To the Actors

This is Father Dan Berrigan speaking from the underground. Your playwright is in good spirits on a beautiful day. I am thinking of you all and of the important event about to be launched by you on our behalf. As I set down these few reflections, I've just finished three months of this absurd underground existence. I don't know exactly what lies at the other end but am convinced that I had better go forward as far as I can.

What specifically would I have to say to you of the cast? I think I've already expressed my feeling about the play to Gordon [Davidson] a few months ago. We all share a certain hope that the Catonsville play might speak to people, might bring them to a more accurate, realistic, and painful sense of things. At the same time we wish to release a capacity of hope and joy. This was the spirit in which we carried off our Catonsville caper, and faced its consequences—consequences which indeed have enlarged since then.

Let me say that in the course of the last five years I have felt a very special hope in regard to Americans. This strange hope grew out of the befouled and violence-ridden atmosphere in which young people were coming into adulthood. At the same time, this atmosphere exerted special pressures, heated things up, and hastened maturity; as a result in certain cases, I saw moral changes of enormous import and quality occurring in these young lives. I saw communities arising very quickly; I had a feeling that such teams or caucuses or communities, connected with an acute political point of view, would offer some clue for the rest of us. And I felt that we had better keep experimenting in this regard, for everything had to be created from whole cloth. It seemed almost as though each of us had been lowered from on high into our existence on wires; we touched ground, the wires were then cut by some hand and there we were. There was a new way of getting born in the world which was special to Americans.

I am speaking of special circumstances, the enormous cultural ferment and the long genetic period of the cold war. Out of the worst came, at least in some measure, the best (and this may be true of our drama, too). Obviously we are unable to reproduce the European experience arising out of religion, or nationalism, or an anti-form of those. Our experience is a rupture of continuity, a little bit like the first morning of the creation of the first man. He rubbed his eyes in the world and awakened, as though there had been no one before him; he was marked by an enormous optimism, as though there had been no failure and no wounds before, as though everything remained to be done, as though almost anything could be done, because he is putting hand and brain to the world for the first time.

The youngest of our members was David Darst, who exemplified Adam awakening in the world. The first man, filled with candor and a sense of surprise and thanksgiving; he proceeded to work as though he bore no shadow, as though everything were possible, as though indeed he was the man who was to make it actual. So this young David lived his life, brought this spirit to us, and died.

The rest of us were enormously more dragged and harried by the experience of the real world. In varying degrees we had covered many continents, many cultures, lived among many peoples, and experienced the blood-ridden fate of man in the twentieth century. So we came to Catonsville with a sense of ourselves and of the world which was neither sour nor disenchanted; still we had passed over that invisible line that Blake calls innocence, into experience. We were singing a different song from David's.

We might recall with a certain envy groups that have arisen in the past years: the Living Theater, the New Theater. We think in their regard of a common discipline, a common view of the world, a common politics, and above all perhaps of a common linking love that grants them an exciting, innovative character. I don't know whether or not this is possible in America except for short periods and small numbers of actors. Maybe we're stuck with short-term efforts, being faithful to a sense of the moment heating things up in our lives and imaginations. Thus we may be able to reproduce some sense of the depth, inwardness and communality that arises in a slower social scene over longer periods. I am speaking again especially of the European dramatic experience and European teams.

It would of course be remarkable if we came to understand that a strong political sense is a clue to making sense of men and women. Much of the stuff that goes by the name theater on and off Broadway has no politics, no real expression in face of the world, is sprayed with the false front of frivolity, amnesia, anomie. Certain productions that are making a great deal of money are infantile in regard to the real world; they contribute only to the public amnesia that afflicts people with dread of the real world. Such work closes the vicious circle in which drama helps retard the moral sense of man, certainly a vicious turnabout from the classical intention of the theater.

How do we help Americans get born, get going, get growing, get moving toward recovery of intention, recovery of what the Greeks would call the true way, the true road, as expressed in Oedipus? But it seems to me that actors, with moral passion and bodily gestures, are in a certain place with regard to the spirit. That is to say, they are exerting pressure against the outer darkness. They are creating and communicating light around their bodies, the light of the human spirit. They are saying something that others are saying in prison and in the underground and in exile and indeed in death. So to be onstage is to be a rather special person these days, to be human in a unique way, to be saying something unique to others. So the connection between resistance and the theater ought to be pondered not merely by actors but by the relationship they strive to establish with their audience as well as by the kind of audience they attract.

You may know that in April of 1970 I made my escape from Cornell surrounded by fifteen thousand students and many FBI agents. The happening occurred during the course of a weekend in celebration of resistance, and especially of the Catonsville Nine. The supposition was that we were all going to jail that weekend. What is delicious in retrospect is that I made my escape through a dramatic troupe, the Bread and Puppet Theater, borrowing one of their large, marvelous puppets of one of the twelve apostles. I proceeded out of the hall bobbing underneath this tremendous papier-mâché and burlap figure, got into a panel truck, and away.

I think it was a metaphor of how one may make his escape into a deeper underground, almost in a Greek mythological sense, into a deeper reality through drama, in such a way that one's escape may become, from another point of view, his return. Theater is not escapism. I am trying to say it is the exact opposite of that. It requires shedding everything that cannot be contained within the strict limits of the definition of human being. One offers this definition by standing in a circle of imaginative protection; the actor's function becomes both the tightening of crisis and the facing together of the consequence of crisis. I would think that in such a way a link is closed between what you are doing onstage and what I am trying to do in the underground. That is to say, we are dramatizing from different points of view, different points of visibility, the teasing and testing aspects of drama. We are hottening things up where we are and then extending our reach so that we are not the only ones saved; so that others get in and under and away with us. It seems to me this makes sense in relationship to the Catonsville play. I cannot imagine an actor entering such a furnace of moral resolve as Catonsville was for us, without changes of a rather serious order occurring within those taking part and those witnessing the act. At least I would hope this would be true.

I wanted to wish you all well and to say that I will be present with you in spirit. So will all the Catonsville people including, I am sure, our dear David, who shares in a special kind of immortality for having desired it so passionately.

And to the Audience

This is your underground playwright speaking. I think quite naturally tonight, and I would have you think, too, of us, the Nine, who at one time sat in your seats, that is to say, led your life—spectators at events, crises, dramas, which we neither initiated nor carried forward. You will witness all of this tonight and will judge for yourselves of our folly and our hope. I would have you think also of where the tide of fortune has carried us in the years since we tested in fire the highest legitimacies of the land, since we tested in fire, in a far closer sense, our own fiber and constancy.

Dear friends, the act of theater, if it is to have meaning for men and women today, is an act, as the Greeks realized, of "mimesis," which we might translate: an act of remembrance. An act which presses upon us a conflict which both renders and records our past and reorders it for the sake of our present soul. The audience, the

Greeks declared, is not to remain unchanged by the working out of tragic intent. The veins of the mind are to be purged of pity and fear, those wasting ills of man's blood which prevent the health of the world flooding in upon him.

The drama is to purge one of pity. He is to be purged only afterward, that is to say, because pity has first welled up a fever of the blood at the sight of visible misfortune. Tonight you are to be purged of pity for us. The drama, it is also said, purges human fear. This is a capital point, too deep to allow for adequate treatment here. But I hope it will become clear that at Catonsville we tried to deal with our fears. For weeks and months we allowed our fears to loom up before us with all their sinister claim on our souls. We faced them down, finally, and purged ourselves in the fire of the parking lot of a remote Maryland town. For we knew that we could not be human and still allow our fears to possess us. And I mean, of course, real fears concerning real threats and punishments, penalties, jail sentences, exiles, separation from family and friends, fear of death itself.

These things have come to pass upon us and are now our daily portion. We now live the consequence of our act, and this can be said of us, that never are we possessed by our fear. And I take it that this fact distinguishes us from the other men and women of our country. The difference is not that we are now convicted felons and others are not. Nor that we are kicked out of America while others enjoy its fruits. Nor that they call us dead men while others live. No, we are free. Free, to this moment, to set our feet in that direction in which conscience and the innocent blood of the victims, men, women, and children, have summoned us.

For you, our friends and hearers and audience and jury, we pray a like boon and favor from the trial of the Catonsville Nine—the purging from your hearts also of the inhabiting demons of pity and fear. Thank you.

11. LETTER TO THE WEATHERMEN

Dear Brothers and Sisters,

Let me express a deep sense of gratitude that the chance has come to speak to you across the underground. It's a great moment; I rejoice in the fact that we can start a dialogue that I hope will continue through the smoke signals, all with a view to enlarging the circle. Indeed the times demand not that we narrow our method of communication but that we enlarge it, if anything new or better is to emerge. (I'm talking out of a set of rough notes; my idea is that I would discuss these ideas with you and possibly publish them later, by common agreement.)

The cold war alliance between politics, labor, and the military finds many Americans at the big end of the cornucopia. What has not yet risen in them is the question of whose blood is paying for all this, what families elsewhere are being blasted, what separation and agony and death are at the narrow end of our abundance. These connections are hard to make, and very few come on them. Many can hardly imagine that all being right with America means that much must go wrong elsewhere. How do we get such a message across to others? It seems to me that this is one way of putting the very substance of our task. Trying to keep connections, or to create new ones. It's a most difficult job, and in hours of depression it seems all but impossible to speak to Americans across the military, diplomatic, and economic idiocies. Yet I think we have to carry our reflection further, realizing that the difficulty of our task is the other side of the judgment Americans are constantly making about persons like ourselves. This determination to keep talking with all who seek a rightful place in the world, or all who have not yet awakened to any sense at all of the real world—this, I think, is the revolution. And the United States perversely and negatively knows it, and this is why we are in trouble. And this is why we accept trouble, ostracism, and fear of jail and of death as the normal condition under which decent men and women are called upon to function today.

Undoubtedly the FBI comes with guns in pursuit of people

ke me because beyond their personal chagrin and corporate ıachismo (a kind of debased esprit de corps; they always get their ıan), there was the threat that the Panthers and the Vietnamese ave so valiantly offered. The threat is a very simple one; we are ıaking connections, religious and moral connections, connections 'ith prisoners and Cubans and Vietnamese, and these connections re forbidden under policies which J. Edgar Hoover is greatly cilled both in enacting and enforcing. They know by now what e are about, they know we are serious. And they are serious bout us. Just as with mortal fear, for the last five years they have nown what the Vietnamese are about, and the Brazilians and ngolese and Guatemalans. We are guilty of making connections, e urge others to explore new ways of getting connected, of etting married, of educating children, of sharing goods and skills, f being religious, of being human, of resisting. We speak for risoners and exiles and that silent, silent majority which is that of ıe dead and the unavenged as well as the unborn. And I am guilty f making connections with you.

By and large the public is petrified of you Weather People. There a great mythology surrounding you—much more than around ıe. You come through in public as embodiment of the public ightmare, menacing, sinister, senseless, and violent: a spin-off of ıe public dread of Panthers and Vietcong, of Latins and Africans, f the poor of our country, of all those expendable and cluttering, nd clamorous lives, those who have refused to lie down and die n command, to perish at peace with their fate, or to drag out their ves in the world as suppliants and slaves.

But in a sense, of course, your case is more complicated because our rebellion is not the passionate consequence of the stigma f slavery. Yours is a choice. It's one of the few momentous choices ı American history. Your no could have been a yes; society ealizes this—you had everything going for you. Your lives could ave been posh and secure; but you said no. And you said it by ttacking the very properties you were supposed to have inherited nd expanded—an amazing kind of turnabout.

Society, I think, was traumatized by your existence, which was ıe consequence of your choice. What to do with Vietcong or 'anthers had never been a very complicated matter, after all. 'hey were jailed or shot down or disposed of by the National

Guard. But what to do with you—this indeed was one hell of a question. There was no blueprint. And yet this question, too, was not long in finding its answer, as we learned at Kent State. That is to say, when the choice between property and human life come up close, the metaphor is once more invariably military. It is lives that go down. And we know now that even if those lives are white and middle-class, they are going to lie in the same gun sights.

The mythology of fear that surrounds you is exactly what the society demands, as it demands more and more mythology, more and more unreality to live by. But it also offers a very special opportunity to break this myth that flourishes on silence and ignorance and has you stereotyped as mindless, indifferent to human life and death, determined to raise hell at any hour or place. We have to deal with this as we go along; but from what values, what mentality, what views of one another and ourselves? Not from a mimicry of insanity of useless rage, but with a new kind of anger which is both useful in communicating and imaginative and slow-burning, to fuel the long haul of our lives.

I'm trying to say that when people look about them for lives to run with and when hopeless people look to others, the gift we can offer is so simple a thing as hope. As they said about Che, as they say about Jesus, some people, even to this day; he gave us hope. So my hope is that you see your lives in somewhat this way, which is to say I hope your lives are about something more than sabotage. I'm certain they are. I hope the sabotage question is tactical and peripheral. I hope indeed that you are uneasy about its meaning and usefulness and that you realize that the burning of properties, whether at Catonsville or Chase Manhattan or anywhere else, by no means guarantees a change of consciousness, the risk always being very great that sabotage will change people for the worse and harden them against enlightenment.

I hope you see yourselves as Che saw himself, that is to say as teachers of the people, sensitive as we must be to the vast range of human life that awaits liberation, education, consciousness. If I'm learning anything it is that nearly everyone is in need of these gifts—and therefore in need of us, whether or not they realize it. I think of all those we so easily dismiss, whose rage against us is an index of the blank pages of their lives, those to whom no meaning or value has ever been attached by politicians or generals or churches or universities or indeed anyone, those whose sons fight the wars, those who are constantly mortgaged and indebted to the consumer system; and I think also of those closer to ourselves, students who are still enchanted by careerism and selfishness, unaware that the human future must be created out of suffering and loss.

How shall we speak to our people, to the people everywhere? We must never refuse, in spite of their refusal of us, to call them our brothers. I must say to you as simply as I know how; if the people are not the main issue, there simply is no main issue and you and I are fooling ourselves, and American fear and dread of change has only transferred itself to a new setting.

Thus, I think a sensible, humane movement operates on several levels at once if it is to get anywhere. So it says communication yes, organizing yes, community yes, sabotage yes—as a tool. That is the conviction that took us where we went, to Catonsville. And it took us beyond, to this night. We reasoned that the purpose of our act could not be simply to impede the war, or much less to stop the war in its tracks. God help us; if that had been our intention, we were fools before the fact and doubly fools after it, for in fact the war went on. Still we undertook sabotage long before any of you. It might be worthwhile reflecting on our reasons why. We were trying first of all to say something about the pernicious effect of certain properties on the lives of those who guarded them or died in consequence of them. And we were determined to talk to as many people as possible and as long as possible afterward, to interpret, to write, and through our conduct, through our appeal, through questioning ourselves again and again to discuss where we were, where we were going, where people might follow.

My hope is that affection and compassion and nonviolence are now common resources once more and that we can proceed on one assumption, the assumption that the quality of life within our communities is exactly what we have to offer. I think a mistake in SDS's past was to kick out any evidence of this community sense as weakening, reactionary, counter-productive. Against this it must be said that the mark of inhuman treatment of humans is a mark that also hovers over us. And it is the mark of a beast, whether its insignia is the military or the movement.

No principle is worth the sacrifice of a single human being. That's a very hard statement. At various stages of the movement some have acted as if almost the opposite were true, as people got purer and purer. More and more people have been kicked out for less and less reason. At one remote period of the past, the result of such thinking was the religious wars, or wars of extinction. At another time it was Hitler; he wanted a ton of purity too. Still another is still with us in the war against the Panthers and the Vietnamese. I think I'm in the underground because I want part in none of this inhumanity, whatever name it goes by, whatever rhetoric it justifies itself with.

When madness is the acceptable public state of mind, we're all in danger, all in danger; for madness is an infection in the air. And I submit that we all breathe the infection and that the movement has at times been sickened by it too.

The madness has to do with the disposition of human conflict by forms of violence. In or out of the military, in or out of the movement, it seems to me that we had best call things by their name, and the name for this thing, it seems to me, is the death game, no matter where it appears. And as for myself, I would as soon be under the heel of former masters as under the heel of new ones.

Some of your actions are going to involve inciting and conflict and trashing, and these actions are very difficult for thoughtful people. But I came upon a rule of thumb somewhere which might be of some help to us: Do only that which one cannot not do. Maybe it isn't very helpful, and of course it's going to be applied differently by the Joint Chiefs of Staff and an underground group of sane men and women. In the former, hypocritical expressions of sympathy will always be sown along the path of the latest rampage. Such grief is like that of a mortician in a year of plague. But our realization is that a movement has historic meaning only insofar as it puts itself on the side of human dignity and the protection of life, even of the lives most unworthy of such respect. A revolution is interesting insofar as it avoids like the plague the plague it promised to heal. Ultimately if we want to define the plague as death (a good definition), a prohuman movement will neither put people to death nor fill the prisons nor inhibit freedoms nor brainwash nor torture enemies nor be mendacious nor exploit women, children, Blacks, the poor. It will have a certain respect for the power of the truth, a power which created the revolution in the first place.

We may take it, I think, as a simple rule of thumb that the revolution will be no better and no more truthful and no more populist and no more attractive than those who brought it into being. Which is to say we are not killers, as America would stigmatize us, and indeed *as America perversely longs us to be*. We are something far different. We are teachers of the people who have come on a new vision of things. We struggle to embody that vision day after day, to make it a reality among those we live with, so that people are literally disarmed by knowing us; so that their fear of change, their dread of life are exorcised, and their dread of human differences slowly expunged.

Instead of thinking of the underground as temporary, exotic, abnormal, perhaps we should start thinking of its implication as an entirely self-sufficient, mobile, internal revival community; the underground as a definition of our future. What does it mean literally to have nowhere to go in America, to be kicked out of America? It must mean—let us go somewhere in America, let us stay here and play here and love here and build here, and in this way join not only those who like us are kicked out also, but those who have never been inside at all, the Blacks and the Puerto Ricans and the Chicanos.

Next, we are to strive to become such men and women as may, in a new world, be nonviolent. If there's any definition of the new man and woman, the man or woman of the future, it seems to me that they are persons who do violence unwillingly, by exceptions. They know that destruction of property is only a means; they keep the end as vivid and urgent and as alive as the means, so that the means are judged in every instance by their relation to the ends. Violence as legitimate means: I have a great fear of American violence, not only in the military and diplomacy, in economics, in industry and advertising; but also in here, in me, up close, among us.

On the other hand, I must say, I have very little fear, from firsthand experience, of the violence of the Vietcong or Panthers (I hesitate to use the word violence), for their acts come from the proximate threat of extinction, from being invariably put on the line of self-defense. But the same cannot be said of us and our history. We stand outside the culture of these others, no matter what admiration or fraternity we feel with them; we are unlike them, we have other demons to battle.

But the history of the movement, in the last years, it seems to me, shows how constantly and easily we are seduced by violence, not only as method but as end in itself. Very little new politics, very little ethics, very little direction, and only a minimum moral sense, if any at all. Indeed one might conclude in despair: the movement is debased beyond recognition, I can't be a part of it. Far from giving birth to the new man, it has only proliferated the armed, bellicose, and inflated spirit of the army, the plantation, the corporation, the diplomat.

Yet it seems to me good, in public as well as in our own house, to turn the question of violence back on its true creators and purveyors, working as we must from a very different ethos and for very different ends. I remember being on a television program recently and having the question of violence thrown at me, and responding—look, ask the question in the seats of power, don't ask it of me, don't ask me why I broke the law, ask Nixon why he breaks the law constantly, ask the Justice Department, ask the racists. Obviously, but for Johnson and Nixon and their fetching ways, Catonsville would never have taken place and you and I would not be where we are today; just as but for the same people SDS would never have grown into the Weather People or the Weather People have gone underground. In a decent society, functioning on behalf of its people, all of us would be doing the things that decent people do for one another. That we are forbidden so to act, forced to meet so secretly and with so few, is a tragedy we must live with. We have been forbidden a future by the forms of power, which include death as the ordinary social method; we have rejected the future they drafted us into, having refused, on the other hand, to be kicked out of America, either by aping their methods or leaving the country.

The question now is what can we create. I feel at your side across the miles, and I hope that sometime, sometime in this mad world, in this mad time, it will be possible for us to sit down face to face, brother to brother, brother to sister, and find that our hopes and our sweat, and the hopes and sweat and death and tears and blood of our brothers and sisters throughout the world, have brought to birth that for which we began.

Shalom to you.

III. Jailhouse Notes

1. FIRST LETTER FROM DANBURY

8/23/70
Danbury
Thursday

Dear ones—

Every time I get this letter underway it gets interrupted by some prisoner or other saying hello, saying thank you, saying we read about Philip & you. So it goes. A very beautiful and sunny day in the yard. I have no duties yet so can work and pray and write as I please, all virtue of Unk Sam.

Well it says in the A.M. *Times* that Philip is to be transferred here. I cannot believe we will both be allowed to stay, so perhaps a transfer for me will be ordered then. There is a certain aura of unease about certain aspects of our present careers. So we shall see.

These are mainly young prisoners, so there is a great deal of good work possible. Either Philip or myself being here will make a great difference.

Please ignore fingerprints and generally poor writing. I am writing on a bench in the open and it is a bit clumsy to begin.

Was wondering if Jerry could send on a few bucks, perhaps 25.00 so I can get a few basics—don't send more as there is no need.

I will append a series of friends' names, asking permission to correspond. Could you please send complete addresses as I lost my address book in the Atlantic somewhere—then I can start the real business here, and get letters off here & there. One of the consolations is being able to get in touch with people again.

There is really not too much new. I am getting land legs after the last months, sorry it had to end, but I guess it was in the stars. The consolation now is knowing there are great days ahead and much work as well.

They have some interesting things in store for me. I'm to have an interview with the chaplain tomorrow and get some facts on Mass and related matters.

If anyone has any books, it would be a favor for many others as well. I have put Betty Bartelme and Jeremy Cott on the list but will have to wait for approval. In time they will inundate us I know.

Some clothes will arrive, not much of any import, except that any watch should be included as well as a gold safety pin. The latter was attached to a medal given me by Paul Mayer's mother—they forbade the pin and let me keep the medal. So it goes, as Kurt Vonnegut would say.

I will sign off, in the fervent hope that all are well & flourishing. I'm sure the weather must be copacetic for the children, I also seem to remember you were going to the camp for a week or so, a gentle & needed diversion.

Undoubtedly I will have news of you.

About 8 young prisoners are in immediate vicinity, one is playing Phil Ochs' "I ain't marching anymore" and singing very well. I ain't either.

Daniel

2. A SERMON FROM PRISON

[The following is the text of a sermon Fathers Philip and Daniel Berrigan were prevented from distributing in the prison at Danbury, Connecticut. It became part of their suit against the federal government for the right to publish without censorship.]

Brothers and Sisters—we, Daniel and Philip Berrigan, speak to you from prison, where we live, if you choose, prisoners of peace—or hostages of war. That is to say, we have been imprisoned because we seriously favor peace and seriously oppose war, facts which made us expendable to the warmakers, liabilities they could not afford.

More than that, we speak to you as prisoners, as men stripped of their rights as human beings, as Christians and as priests. We cannot speak freely, cannot write or publish, cannot reach those who need us and cannot meet people whose lives and political convictions are enmeshed with our own. We have no pulpit but the one you provide, no audience but you. And we enter further jeopardy even in speaking to you.

We are, in effect, men without a country for the duration of our sentences, exiles-at-home, whose citizenship has been suspended until the omnipotent state feels that punishment has sufficiently reeducated us to conformity, as most good citizens are conformists.

Yet, as this message indicates, we insist upon free speech, insist upon a pulpit, insist upon even a congregation, since we dare to speak for prisoners everywhere, political or otherwise. Like ourselves, they are voiceless, silenced, oppressed, treated as those who have no grasp upon human stature or dignity. Yet contrary to the courts that sentenced them and the society that ostracized them, we believe that from their ranks—as God writes straight with crooked lines—will come new perception and compassion, new experience and energy, to replace the tired and rigid mediocrity which condemned them.

As we face you through these few words, a critical question occupies us, a question public enough to occupy you as well.

Why are we in jail, and why are there with us, Panthers and Chicanos, draft resisters and draft-file burners, plus poor men who have broken the law as an only way of asserting their right to exist? Because, we would suggest, we acted sanely in an insane society, because we felt the futility of peaceful words without peaceful deeds, because we rejected complicity with a culture and a power structure which idolizes power and privilege, and degrades human life.

We are in jail, we insist, because we would neither remain silent nor passive before the pathology of naked power, which rules our country and dominates half the world, which shamelessly wastes resources as well as people, which leaves in its wake racism, poverty, foreign exploitation, and war. In face of this we felt, free men cannot remain free and silent, free men cannot confess their powerlessness by doing nothing.

We spoke out, committed civil disobedience, and went to jail because the peace hangs senselessly and precariously upon weapons costing billions to build and billions to improve—weapons which become more useless as we add to their destructive force. With this money we could have fed the world's people. Half the children on earth go to bed hungry—millions more have retarding and stunting protein deficiencies. Instead of building the peace by attacking injustices like starvation, disease, illiteracy, political and economic servitude, we spend a trillion dollars on war since 1946, until hatred and conflict have become the international preoccupation. Indeed, following our quality of leadership, 70 percent of the nations are either now at war, or preparing seriously for war.

To remain prosperous, America defaces its countrysides, fouls its air and water, makes its cities unlivable, and, as ultimate irony, pollutes its oceans with surplus safety, ten thousand bombs of obsolete nerve gas in thin and vulnerable containers.

Our institutions and the rules governing them no longer promote the best interests of anyone, including those who keep them stagnant for personal gain. Churches and synagogues fear the Scriptures, and fear living them; universities undertake war-related research, even as they refuse to lead the young; business puts profit over human life and welfare, while legislatures are filled with those who, for the most part, are vote-getters, rather than critics of war policy and servants of human welfare.

America fights a stupid and genocidal war in Indochina, mostly because we don't know how to turn off the bloody spigot we have opened. That is to say, we are powerless to inquire why it is easier to continue the slaughter than to stop it, why the historical cult of violence has become the mainstay of policy—both foreign and domestic, or why our economy so requires warmaking that perpetual war has united with expanding profits as the chief national purpose.

In face of such bewilderment, which has seized and taken captive our national sanity, the government remains impotent. First, because government is a coalition of big business, big finance, and big military, whose rapacity has become policy. And secondly, because the silent middle class, threatened from below by the poor, and from above by the rich and their government, is morally absorbed, immobilized. Only some students, Blacks, a cross section of the poor, and a few radical Christians trouble the government by questioning the ruling class, and by attempting to hold it accountable. In response, the government is powerless to redress, powerless in fact to do other than remain deaf to their concerns, their sacrifices, even their deaths. It can only ridicule them, silence them in jail, or crush them.

We greet you at a time roughly coinciding with Yom Kippur, the Jewish Day of Atonement, and the Christian feast of St. Francis. During these days, Jews fast for a day, review the ninety-nine sins, and humbly promise a life renewed by service of their brothers. Christians look to the Little Brother of Assisi, who reverenced all life, desiring only to sow love where there was hate. Both traditions shed light upon our predicament. Peacemaking has now become more than moral and political duty—it is a condition for human survival.

Yet contemporary peacemaking must go far beyond acknowledgment of failure to one's God and one's community, as the High Holy Days require; or the personal love that Francis lived. It must resist the powers of this world, the institutions of domination and their chieftains, whose wealth and position give them control over the resources of the world and the lives and deaths of human beings.

What we plead for, what we are attempting to live, is the truth of hope, which asserts that men & women have been made new by Christ, that they can use freedom responsibly, that they can build a world uncursed by war, starvation, and exploitation. Such hope, once created and defended, leads inevitably to nonviolent revolution.

A hard question arises—when does opposition to unjust law become the measure of a human, and therefore moral, and political duty? It seems to us that the time for resistance has come, as surely as your lives and ours have been threatened by senseless obedience to senseless laws. It seems to us that communities must control Selective Service (by putting them out of business); they must encourage and harbor military deserters; they must refuse taxes that are war-related; they must withdraw from war industry and war profiteering. They must even think of destroying war ordnance and horror weapons, taking every precaution in so doing, to protect human life. Finally, they must strive to bring the business of this nation to a halt, since nothing educates the mandarins like seeing their profits jeopardized. In a word, one must build the peace by first striking at the causes of war and rendering them powerless.

"Peacemaking is hard, hard almost as war." It seems to us that, when we understand how hard war is, we understand the obligation to make peace. There will be no moral equivalent of war until we engage the price of war—technological terror, scorched earth, millions of dead Indochinese, young American lives snuffed out, a ruined society in Southeast Asia, untold billions of treasure wasted—sorrow, despair, desperation, rage. If we understand modern war, we understand the effort that peace requires. And we settle for nothing but total peace.

We choose peace, not in rhetoric alone, but in truth, love, in risk, suffering, in every element of our lives. Even if that meant loss of possession, public disgrace, prison, death. To lose that others might gain, to be imprisoned that others might be free, to die that others might live, this is the stuff of life, this is humanity in its fullest glory.

The Master so spoke, following the great Jewish prophets: "This is my commandment, love one another as I have loved you. There is no greater love than this, that a man should lay down his life for his friends. You are my friends, if you do what I command you." (John 15:13–14).

And Isaiah: "For a yoke that burdened them, a yoke on their shoulder, and the rod of their taskmaster you have smashed. . . . For every boot that tramped in battle, every cloak rolled in blood, will be burned as fuel for flames. For a child is born to us, a son is given us; upon his shoulder dominion rests. They name him Wonder-Counsellor, God-Hero, Father-Forever, Prince of Peace." (Isaiah 9:1–4).

3. A LETTER TO JUDGE ROSZEL THOMSEN

[The following letter was addressed by Daniel Berrigan from prison to Judge Roszel Thomsen, the federal judge who sentenced the Catonsville Nine.]

My Dear Judge Roszel Thomsen:

It may seem strange—it may also be unacceptable—that I write Your Honor, after the events of last summer. I have no intention of troubling you, let me say at the outset, with an apologia for my four months underground. It may be a source of somber satisfaction to those who hunted me down with such ardor that I have at length entered on the life of a convicted felon, safely separated from society in consequence of his crime. They may continue to wonder that one such as I, with honors and pride of place at his disposal, could have decided upon so mad a course as Catonsville opened. At the same time, I venture to hope that even my opponents may concede a grudging sort of admiration for a man who (1) refused at every point to seize upon, or to urge upon others, the tools of violence, either to defend or to further his beliefs, and who (2) risked further legal jeopardy in order to draw attention to the continuing war, the mounting despair of good men, and the fate of political prisoners in America.

In a sense, Judge Thomsen, the foregoing is beside the point of this letter. In another sense, it is a necessary prelude: I am trying to suggest the continuity of moral purpose that joins Catonsville to my four months underground. I wanted to declare once more that legal means of redress were exhausted, that protest as a social tool of change was dead as a doornail, that the dead were being multiplied on schedule, that thousands of victims had perished since Catonsville and our trial, that no one in power seemed to care, since the victims were drawn mostly from the powerless and poor of both societies. And who finally is poorer or more powerless than the dead? I must speak for them. In the words of our dear David Darst, "We had to cry out." And how can we silence that cry, as long as death-dealing remains the acceptable way of dealing with human conflict—and our faith tells us of another way to which we must be faithful, at whatever cost?

So I am in prison at last. Determined, as I can assure you, to make the best of a bad situation, to live, as a friend urged me, "As a man there—for the men." Which is not to be so translated that my brother and I become resigned merely to "doing good time," turning away from suffering and injustice, making hay for ourselves.

I recall often in this regard the words you addressed to the two of us at our sentencing. You urged us to put our gifts to work in prison, helping in whatever way to rehabilitate the prisoners—especially the younger ones. The sincerity that infused your words struck me then, and stays with me. Though we stood at diametrically opposite poles of society, of experience, of office—you as judge over our fate, we as convicted and powerless felons—still I felt that an arc of communion was struck, was reaching out to unite us—a sense of common decency and concern. You had never before, I think, been called upon to vindicate American law under such vexing circumstances; we had never before the war been accused, let alone convicted, of crime. After that moment, and your judgment upon us, our paths, which a tempestuous destiny had joined, drew apart once more; the two brothers went their way to prison, you went on, to the day-by-day dispensation of justice—a thankless and wrenching task indeed in the America of the seventies.

But you had spoken to us. And I took you seriously, perhaps more seriously than you could expect. On the one hand our training disposes us to take seriously (overseriously, our critics would have it) the command of authority, civil or religious. "To take seriously"—that is, as I understand it, neither to obey nor to disobey as a robot. On the other hand, if I may go more nearly to the heart of our attitude, we have tried to make our life a search for the will of God. We did not judge that His will could lead us so far and then abandon us at the prison door. No, if we were to be locked up, that episode would have its reasons too, its good sense, its ministry, its unlocking of new insights and resources. All this I believe, in the dark way one believes today—part trusting, part dread, an atmosphere of distress of heart, indignation and nausea of spirit, over wrongs that refuse to be righted, and so must simply be lived with. And yet we believe that, out of the worst, some good may come, if we will only consent to endure and be faithful.

So I have tried during these past months to listen, to counsel, to be patient, to question myself and my fellow prisoners here, to understand—all with your advice in mind. And I have come upon certain insights, which I venture to predict the future will serve to vindicate. May I share these with you?

(1) It seems to me that the rehabilitation of criminals is linked to the question of moral change in society. This truth seems, on the fact of things, painfully obvious; it is nonetheless the heart of the matter. I mean that our prisons do not rehabilitate, because our society itself is destitute of a vision of man. Ours is not at depth a failure of money or means. It is a failure of authority, whether of church or state, in high or low places, to take its own tradition seriously—to pursue it, to ponder it in season and out—to embody it—whether the tradition in question is the Constitution of the United States or the gospel of Christ.

In this sense, prisoners who grow conscious (my word for rehabilitation) find themselves in the uneasy position of those everywhere who grow conscious—whether they be war resisters, Blacks, the poor, priests or ministers or rabbis. Such men and women tend to see themselves across all differences of origin or need in roughly the same light. None of these wants to make his peace with America today—whether with war policies, the draft, racism, selfish economics, a somnolent church. In this sense, to be rehabilitated means that one gets reborn—from the status of criminal to the status of resister. One rejects the definition conferred by the law, in the travail to which imprisonment subjects him. One comes to see that the consumer society, bent more on war than on peace, more on the creation of debilitating hungers than the satisfying of truly human needs, has, even in defining crime and exacting punishment, attempted to define one's life. That is to say, one is a bad or faulty consumer, he has refused to play the rules of a bad game (at Danbury he is in prison because he passed bad checks, or stole cars, or counterfeited, or used or sold drugs). Such men upset the applecart, or steal from it, or adulterate its goods and services. But the vast majority never think to ask who owns the cart (United Fruit?), who harvests the apples (exploited migrants?), whether the apples are sprayed with lethal DDT. At every point, I am trying to say, grave questions arise when one awakens to a sense of life today; the fruit of the garden, once consumed, issues in political and human insight of the widest implications—or indeed in further blindness.

But suppose a few prisoners were to enter upon such reflections, to use their time well, to assume responsibility for their future, to read, to be exposed to books and ideas, to strengthen their bonds with whatever was humane, compassionate, and courageous in the community outside. Would such prisoners not begin to pose questions about the quality of American life—politics, education, war, race, religion, family, environment, community? Would you agree that their rehabilitation was underway—and that, short of such an awakening, nothing worth speaking about had happened to them? No matter how long they were imprisoned, how carefully scrutinized, how finally approved as reformed?

But if prisoners were to be born anew, if prisons were really working as centers of renewal and education, I submit that two things would be occurring concretely: First, prisoners would return to society beset with doubts about America's conduct in the world and their own future conduct in America, if that conduct were to be no more than an obedient cycle (consumer–taxpayer–draftee–churchgoer) that kept them (in jail or out) prisoners of society; secondly, prisoners would be resolved to take responsibility for their lives and the lives of their brothers and sisters. In them, sane politics and authentic religion would meet, against all the expectation of those who imprisoned them (against their own expectation perhaps, as well).

(2) The change I speak of (the aptitude to question life and accept and enact change in one's conduct) actually gets underway in very few cases. Moreover, it could be justly said that such change is the exception everywhere, not only in prisoners, but in priests and judges as well. What needs underscoring here is

the deceitfulness of a prison system that exacts mechanical conformity, scrutinizes and searches out every detail of prisoners' lives, through censorship, humiliating "strip search," limitations of visitors, sexual denial, extends the bland and boring through time, space, books, food, work, play, religion, creates childish permissiveness at the center and paranoia at the edges—and calls the resultant state of things rehabilitation. No, I must respectfully but firmly submit, all such enactments and arrangements constitute in themselves, from any human point of view, cruel and unusual punishment.

Obviously I speak of one instance only—Danbury Prison is not the New York Tombs, nor are we the despairing who shook those walls, literally, in order to break the circle of their torment. But we are men, too, and prisoners, and in our eyes it makes no great difference that our prison is a scene of moral and mental retardation, rather than a mock-up of Dante's hell. I am not even certain that hell, like heaven, does not have many dwellings. Or that in some of them, the punishment is not the methodical bloody dismemberment of the living. In our prison, punishment is so simple and subtle a fact as this: "At Danbury, nothing human is allowed to happen." One could not say truthfully that here men are subject to overt cruelty or corporal mishandling. Rather they are systematically robbed of their human potential, of education and human relationships, a cruelty which I assure you is even harder to diagnose and cure than the overt kind.

(3) There is from such a prison, in Sartre's phrase, no exit. The exits his drama speaks of are, I think, simply the avenues of human growth available in society to those who wish to be human. We look at the youth of America, at their valid expectations, their hopes for the future, and we take our cues from them. What do they look for, what do the best of them wish to create? I think in the main they look for two things: education and exposure to society. With such tools they "habilitate themselves" to a future which deserves the name "human." They ready themselves, soul and body, for their community—to *become* their society, to become responsible, wise, compassionate, skilled, nonviolent in conduct and ethos, generous of heart, idealistic and practical in action. They prepare to innovate in political life, in professional life, in church life. They

wish to transform their society by becoming a viable part of it. They wish "a chance in life," as our parents used to say, "A better chance than we had."

(4) Now it is just this chance, I submit, that is being denied to prisoners. The denial strikes hardest, in the nature of things, against young prisoners. Little education, even less exposure to society; the systematic breaking of those bonds to other minds, to other lives; a break which in fact breaks them to pieces; the pernicious opposite process to what official jargon loves to call "rehabilitation."

May I now, after these reflections, try to be as practical as I can, both with regard to present failure and possible breakthrough?

On December 15, 1969, a statement was issued by federal correctional authorities having to do with inmate furloughs. The statement is generous and thoughtful. It provides for released time outside prison, up to thirty days, to be spent in "selected family, religious, educational, social, civic, recreational activities, when such participation will facilitate . . . transition from institution to community."

On September 11, 1970, the statement was published at Danbury —some nine months after its promulgation.

One inmate of my acquaintance applied for such a furlough to his case worker and was told, "You write the application, I'll refuse it." Prospects that the decree will be put to any use are not good—I know of no case at Danbury where such a furlough has been granted. The prisoners are cynical; they speak of election time. Who knows if they are wrong? Does the Bureau of Prisons want such a statement on paper, to prove to interested outsiders that a human policy is in effect—one that would never, or only very rarely, be actualized?

Let us look at the prior record of Danbury, as it touches on work and educational release programs. Such efforts were in effect here for years, "to minimize the offender's alienation from his family and community life." At present, out of 750 inmates, some 5 attend classes outside the walls, some 15 take part in work programs outside. No more. The figures are hardly reassuring. As evidence of the official determination to rehabilitate inmates, they become even less encouraging if one considers the concomitant large-scale growth of prison industries. But more of this later.

How would you or I set about defining education today, as the term applies to prisoners? You will have your ideal in mind. I will have mine. But I am sure we would concur along certain lines. There would occur to our minds certain men and women we love and admire—models of ethical purity, awareness, greatness of soul—persons incapable of meanness, hatred, racism, violence, selfishness, bent to the task of binding up the nation into a beloved community. On the other hand, there occur to us the bitter fruits of miseducation, as these touch American conduct and corrupt our very souls; the repression of legitimate dissent, the political appeal to worst instincts, fear and hatred of differing views and styles of life, dread of change, the ambiguous blessings of religion granted to nationalistic frenzies. And so on and so on.

But how shall we educate others to goodness, to a sense of one another, to a love of the truth? And more urgently, how shall we do this in a bad time? I have given many years of my life to such questions, so has my brother; so, in a different profession, have you.

The difference in our views is not, I venture, a matter of substance. Still, though you have sent men and women to prison, my brother and I have lived the life of prisoners—a different matter entirely. What have we learned that may be of value to both you and us? First of all, at Danbury, as elsewhere, the prison situation is becoming daily more volatile. Prisoners are linking their fate to the "outsiders" of society—the poor, from whom they are mainly drawn, the Blacks, the war resisters, the minority peoples. They know that official definitions and sanctions against crime are applied with all rigor to the poor; they sense in fact that the worst crime of all in America is simply to be poor. Moreover, in places like Danbury, the numbers of younger, better-educated, more intelligent prisoners are growing, mainly due to drug-law enforcement. So when improvements are made, almost entirely aimed at physical comfort or distraction, they are written off as pacifying measures, not touching the heart of the matter.

What such inmates long for and speak most often of, and

almost despair achieving, is some control over their lives, some voice in policies that affect them nearly, some personal enlargement of choices—about what they will read or write, study, work at; some connection with friends and family beyond five hours a month; some chance of visiting home (once or twice a year); some human exchange with guards and officials. Some recognition in fact that they are human, have dignity, desperately long for a measure of autonomy and freedom, hate their present existence with all their strength, and see no way out beyond mere animal endurance.

And *keep in mind*, please, this is Danbury, the place where, so they say, innovation is a working principle and the best interests of prisoners are seriously taken into account. Here work is meaningful and education rich and varied. So they say. But those who say so are not prisoners.

With them I must fervently agree, for the facts are something else again. May I be specific?

Almost half the inmates here work at a phenomenon called "Prison Industries." According to a recent annual report of this federal bureau, its object is to provide "a large work force of semiskilled and unskilled laborers." Purportedly, the plan makes sense, taking into account as it does, "the relatively low educational background of the inmates at Danbury" (a few years past; nine and a half grades). Could there be a clearer statement of correctional priorities (industrial over educational), or a clearer sign that the educational level of large numbers of inmates is *not* to be advanced during prison years? Or, given stated norms of production, a clearer subordination of prisoners' welfare to consumer and military needs?

Last year, Prison Industries returned the U. S. Treasury some $5 million in profits. A sizable percentage of these profits accrued from war-related industries at Danbury, where cable assemblies are made for missiles and shipped to domestic bases and allies abroad. Top wages for inmate industrial workers is less than fifty cents per hour; in their case, no minimal wage laws apply. Thus, in effect, prisoners supply a domestic work force for the government and its current war and war preparation. Prisoners are stripped of the rights which are slowly being applied, and in principle belong, to all Americans, whether Black, Indians, or migrants.

I searched in the prison library for some evidence that money was being spent for books or periodicals. There is no such evidence. There are literally no magazine subscriptions. I could not find that in the past 15 years a single book had been purchased for the library—or indeed that a fund existed for such a purpose.

In the education department, for the first time, a course of study (psychology) is being offered this year aimed at inmates of college level. The vast majority of courses reflect faithfully the principle I quoted earlier: production, through the prisons, of a semiskilled or unskilled labor force for the society. Thus the courses offered are aimed at keeping factory hands at the lathe; they freeze men in the cycle from which they entered prison. There is little understanding, however, and less exploring of the idea that education should enable a prisoner to know his world, his society, the forces that shape and misshape life, to become wise or a lover of truth, to better his mind, his lot, his life.

At least such conditions force me to think at a deeper level. One must ask, since education demands a human and (at least relatively) free environment, can real education occur behind bars?

Let me sketch a proposal, to which the above question has led me.

I should like to be released from Danbury for a thirty-day furlough according to the terms of the policy statement I referred to. My purpose, to visit officials of the Bureau of Correction, and university and college campuses in the East. I would like to recruit teachers for a proposed new Halfway Educational Center; I already am in touch with three or four such professors, competent in their field; they would be eager to take part in such an experiment. I should like to be able to offer them a position beginning with next September. They would form, together with me (possibly my brother) and some enlightened prison official, the faculty of this new venture.

The venture would begin as soon as I ended my furlough and returned to Danbury. We would immediately form an experimental community of some ten or twelve prisoners, plus an official (also prepared to teach), plus my brother and myself. We would begin by meeting each day for one or two hours at a place outside the prison. The place is unimportant, except that the atmosphere of prison be exorcised—with all its guards, counts, buzzers, and bars. I think a rural farmhouse nearby would be ideal. Gradually, our time outside would be extended, as the community discovered itself and settled into studies and work. By next summer, a point would be reached when we would be living together, responsible for our own lives and surroundings—working, cleaning, repairing, gardening. Then we would be ready to welcome our faculty; until then, we would augment our members with the services of two or three volunteer faculty members from neighboring colleges, the course would be set up by the community itself, prisoners, officials, visiting professors.

It seems essential, in addition, that the discipline of such a group be set up by the members themselves. They would agree in principle neither to attempt escape, nor to introduce drugs, to abide by a daily timetable of manual work, classes, and study. I would also hope to have available to us the part-time services of a psychiatrist or psychologist sympathetic to such a venture as ours.

In addition to the foregoing, I suggest that an exhaustive review of the educational program at Danbury is long overdue. The welfare of the general populace has been subverted over the years until it is subject to the most questionable goals of the society. At present, as I suggested above, education stands at the lowest priority, and the industries, comprising boring piecework, slave labor in fact, is accorded prime place. The inmates are viewed in the main as so many factory hands; underpaid and undervalued, integers at disposal of social and economic engineers.

If I speak harshly of these things, believe me, it is because of conditions here. Men lose heart while the rhetoric of rehabilitation goes on. All criticism of sacrosanct regulations is forbidden under heavy penalty; mail is closely censored, visitors are permitted only a few hours a month. In prison disciplinary infractions, there is no access to trial by peers or to outside legal aid. Were I to protest any of the above I would risk being summarily transferred to a high-security prison. And this would occur, even though I were protesting conditions no court would permit in the case of any American—save America's prisoners.

Can you imagine, Judge Thomsen, the effect upon yourself or your sons were you or they so cast adrift, so isolated, so forbidden human intercourse, your life reduced to a limbo over which the law had raised its decree—Nothing Shall Happen Here. Suppose further that the public cover for all this were a rhetoric at once stern and sycophantic, proclaiming that you were being transformed (out of sight, out of mind) into a new man, fit for a new society?

We need to put an end to such pious words, concealing as they do such mortifying and ugly facts. We must begin to act as though humans were redeemable. When such redemption occurs, it is because a spark of hope and love has awakened in their hearts, and burst into flame. No one can strike or cherish the flame but a prisoner. Do we believe this? If we do, we must offer to prisoners, not the punishment of suspended animation, but access to riches of mind and spirit that make life worth living anywhere.

Most Americans do not share such ideas. We seem to believe that it is less than criminal for the Department of Justice to own hundreds of acres of Connecticut countryside, and still to pen some seven hundred men, like cattle, in two or three of these acres (including all living facilities, for housing, eating, classrooms). We seem to place faith in the healing power of pens, cells, cages, bars, guards, and the inevitable spiritual attitudes they give rise to—fear, time-serving, suspicion, anger, despair, and inner violence—on both sides. We seem to believe that factories are more productive of human growth than classes, teachers, books—or even open farm work. So we build (at Danbury or elsewhere) industrial prisons within prison. We seem to believe that low pay, little training, or education, separation from spouses, children, and friends, will bring healing change to an offender, and that such treatment as is commonly accorded and accepted as decent "outside," will not.

No, Judge Thomsen, if your words to us were serious, if moreover you seriously believe that, in sending men and women to jail, you enable them to change their lives instead of losing them—to despair, boredom, and death of the spirit—if this is true, I submit my reflections are worthy of your attention. We must spend time, money, talent in the dismemberment of the prison empire. We must substitute for it humane groupings of inmates, and dedicated specialists—instead of the conglomerates of low talent and special interest who presently, in such abundance, batten off the misery of others, adamant against all or any change. We need to substitute for the crime of punishment a sense of the true potential of the people. We need to help others give the lie to the lie that is forced on them as a fact of life—that it is criminal in America to be poor; that once poor, always poor, and potentially criminal. We need to believe that prisoners can form their own communities, be responsible for one another, be fiercely sensitive, decent and generous toward one another. We need to spur these communities until they are a reality—instead of the depressing malfunctioning anthills of criminals and oppressors which now deface our landscape. We need to begin treating others as though they were our brothers and sisters, since brotherhood is at least as much our need as theirs.

Admittedly, Judge Thomsen, my ideas are inchoate. I judged it best to put them down, imperfectly, as they are conceived and expressed. The time is short, the future of many depends on our courage and vision. And this is why I have written you, because you first addressed us on these matters, in a sense placed a trust and responsibility on us. Taking you seriously as I did, I wish now to learn how seriously you take us.

So this letter. Will you read and ponder it, and intervene with other authorities, so that something may come of it? We await your answer eagerly.

Please pardon the calligraphy. Conditions here are indeed somewhat primitive—but perhaps this gives such a letter a mark of authenticity.

I even dare hope someday to see you again (conceivably at Danbury?) to speak of these matters. If not, to exchange letters will be a privilege.

Sincerely, gratefully,

Daniel Berrigan, S.J.

4. A LETTER TO J. EDGAR HOOVER

[The following letter, in a slightly different form, was read into the Congressional Record by Representative William R. Anderson of Tennessee.]

Danbury, Connecticut
May 16, 1971

Dear Mr. Hoover:

The removal of my name from the federal indictments in the Harrisburg case affords me the opportunity to address you. Such an opportunity could not be said to exist while I lay under the jeopardy of the law, as announced by yourself last November. So I hasten to write you while I enjoy the status of a disinterested party.

I ask you to recall, lest the above sound ironic, the "progress" of my case. According to your November announcement I was a ringleader in a spectacular plot. Then, at a later date, I was shunted to the outer circle of guilt; my status was reduced to that of "unindicted conspirator." Finally I was purged of that nebulous criminality. I was declared, out of court, not so much an innocent person as a non-person, with respect to this case.

But this letter, with all respect, concerns yourself as well as me. You are much in the news these days. In a sense, and with no intemperate irony, it seems that our roles have been strangely reversed. A year ago I was the object of a purposeful manhunt by your agents. The hunt was concluded successfully; I was delivered into custody. Now, the national media, political officeholders, even certain highly placed agents of your household, declare or imply that your public usefulness has ended. The defense offered by your superiors and colleagues is tepid; your removal from office is regarded in many circles as an event urgently required, as some say, "for the welfare of the bureau"; or others, "for the welfare of the nation."

Thus our present situation, yours and mine. It may be fitting, before I continue, to outline what I do *not* intend to discuss in this letter.

(1) I will not needle or prod you in a spirit of revenge. Indeed I

have a serious quarrel with your misuse of authority, your intemperate and illegal "revelations" of last November. But, luckily for me, your accusations have not stood. Their untruth is evident, and I am content.

(2) Neither does this letter announce a suit against you for defamation of character. Such an action holds no appeal for me. My honor depends on no settlement from you.

(3) Nor do I wish to enter into your motives of last November, or of any other occasion. Whether vindictiveness, pique, or outraged ego have governed your attitudes toward myself and others (many of them respected public figures) is not mine to conclude. In the final analysis this matter rests between your conscience and God.

When these matters are put aside, I believe the ground is cleared for fruitful discussion. I would like to believe that the spirit of nonviolence may govern your pen and mine. Further, that this same spirit may create its own ground rules and style: no hidden plays, no invisible writing, no subtle or sweet revenge. Rather, fidelity on both sides to the saying of St. Ignatius, "That the truth might appear." A truth that neither of us is in possession of, but that might be granted us because each is open to its demands.

Perhaps, in this spirit, we can (in a manner of speaking) destroy those "files" which opponents are tempted to accumulate against one another. Let us keep no memory bank of one another's delicts or sins. I would like simply to share with you certain experiences, views of life, impressions of America and of American prisons. I would like to reflect on your role and mine in society, on conscience, on religious tradition, on war and peace, on crime and punishment. On these subjects and whatever others you may wish to pursue.

A persistent suggestion was made to me during the past days that I should urge you in this letter to resign from office as soon as may be convenient. I rejected this counsel with only small hesitation; it seemed to me both inappropriate in principle and dubious in value. By what right should I intervene in such a matter, especially when I am convinced that your replacement would offer no solution to the problems which bedevil us? Indeed if 51 percent of Americans believe that you should be replaced in office, it is not because they object in principle to spies, provocateurs, defamation of character, or trials through public media. It would be difficult to discover indeed whether Americans judged you had gone too far, or not far enough, in these matters.

It is of small interest to me therefore whether you choose to continue in office or not. In such offices as yours, replacements are at hand; qualities of inflexibility, sternness, moral conformity so permeate the national character as to throw up, with regularity, men who will do honor to such offices.

What the nature of that office has become under your guiding genius continues to intrigue many. It even offers me a kind of chilling comfort to reflect that being a prisoner in America today is a way of anticipating the America of, say, 1984. You and others are even now creating that America. In prison our civil and human rights are curtailed or suspended. Our mail is censored, public speech is cut off, access to family and friends is restricted, dissent summarily (some would say brutally) dealt with. We prisoners are in fact (I am a veritable Quixote in pursuit of positive thinking) the subject of an important paramedical experiment. We today, America tomorrow! Authorities are persuaded that the amputation of human rights is of benefit to delinquents; so they proceed to put saw and ax to the body social. Better a healthy basket case than a sound troublemaker! Or again, if a delinquent is rehabilitated by cutting back his dignity, can not society be reformed by a like radical surgery? Crutches and prosthetics will then be no embarrassment to anyone; a gimp will join a limping society. Dissent will be a dim memory of early heroes and their happenings, America will have created her final revolution against all revolution, including her own.

I do believe this process is already underway. By, say 1984, the ineffable benefits of my present existence ought to be available, by law, to all Americans. That is to say, their social intercourse will be monitored, their speech tapped, their access to family and friends controlled, their urges toward dissent summarily (some would say brutally) dealt with.

Undoubtedly a larger talent is required to get such machinery in motion than to fall under its gears. Not talent alone, but organization, moneys, charismatic purpose, morality. My congratulations. You can at present point to all sorts of evidence that the machine is in motion and functioning to satisfaction. One has only to think of the army of trained agents (many of them religiously afire), of access to the Congress, to the President, to the media. As or me, I have fallen under your gears. I am officially reduced to ilence and can address you only under the legal fiction of a court ction. I am moreover smeared with the large brush you wielded last November. Alas for me, no American brush cleans quite as well as it lirties—a fact well known to yourself. Removal of charges does not eave one untarred. The mark you traced against my name remains a 'yes, but . . ." a question mark. Bravo for you.

I am thus a specific instance of a general trend, an American trend or which credit, within measure, must be accorded to you. Let me ry to define the trend. It moves our country in a single direction—oward the death of freedom, which is to say the death of men and vomen as we have known them and nurtured them, the death of America. Of the reality of this trend, I am one example (a criminal one), of its success.

But let us be exact. Large as your role has been in creating the first tages of the New America, still your part has about it a necessary nodesty. One must admit that, if you had not been available to the America of our century, American genius would have created omeone like you. Not so skillful or single-minded perhaps, not ifted with that longevity which has enabled you for so many years o be warden and spokesman for the conscience, the fears, and opes of a turbulent and tortured nation.

You are not, in other words, to be confused with the direction America has chosen. But you have sensed the direction, have egitimatized it, bestowed on it the sacrosanct name of law and rder, won for it the blessing of the churches. The nation called you, nd you responded—with nearly heroic constancy. Political roublemakers, the angry and disenchanted, the clairvoyant and leviant—these you unmasked, punished, put away.

By such crusades, so the reasoning went, Americans might become t length the people they so fervently longed to be—a people of nnocence, of conscience, of benevolence.

One would not be so blind as to deny that your crusades, in eculiarly American terms, have produced "results." You were able o announce, year after year, a rising tide of crime, and to confront t. You and the bureau stood at the open end of a stinking ornucopia, as the "criminals" poured out. You were empowered ot only to seize on them and bring them to justice, but to help America define their crimes as well. Crimes against the sound dollar, against General Motors, against laissez-faire, against national security, against NATO and SEATO, against war, against racism. The crime, in many instances, of defining or aiding or abetting or conspiring toward a vision that was in conflict with yours, and therefore in conflict with America. And therefore criminal.

You have grown in that effort, and I am in prison, and Americans are not yet the people they long to become. In fact, you and I, for vastly different reasons, might agree somberly that America is further than ever from realizing that vision. The people are distempered, ridden with fear, distrustful of one another, itchy to take and to inflict blows. Their faces reassure neither themselves nor the world; God-fearing and bellicose, spartan and self-indulgent, puritanical and prurient. Alas, some would claim that the immaculate purity of the goal is all but lost in the welter of impure means. Among which means, some would suggest, must be numbered Vietnam, Kent State, informers, misuse of grand juries, violence of the FBI.

This impurity besetting the nation and besotting its soul is, let me confess, the clue to my peculiar pride. I believe that the means and the goal must be one. So, in America, in 1971, I had rather be a prisoner on my own terms, than a President on yours.

This summer I will have completed a year of my prison term. I will appear before a parole board to give evidence of my rehabilitation. I should like you to be the first to know that I am indeed rehabilitated. This year I have counseled and befriended young prisoners, helped conduct classes in such books as the gospel according to St. Matthew, Gandhi's *Autobiography*, *Gulliver's Travels*, Erikson's *Young Luther*. I have worked in the prison dental clinic, meditated on my crime and punishment, celebrated Mass; in every way I know I have lived according to the best urgings of my soul. Thus my fiftieth year has come and gone in the urgent effort to habilitate my life to the tempo and hope of humanity.

I have no hope at all that this program will be found satisfactory to my keepers. In every likelihood, I will be informed that my prison term is to be extended to the maximum. The decision I accept in advance; it is predictable, and in the logic of present-day America, right and just. I have not, after all, murdered children under military orders, nor tortured prisoners, nor napalmed women, nor laid waste a foreign culture.

My crime in comparison with such incidents of war is plenary; I have burned papers instead of children. Let us rejoice together that justice can distinguish criminal priests from military heroes.

You will pardon me, however, if a vexing question sticks in my mind. It concerns you. You have publicly accused me of plotting crimes against humans and property; your accusation denied me a hearing or a trial. How, I ask myself, does American justice apply in your case?

The answer is a simple one. Justice does not apply. The bold assurance with which you spoke against me is proof that you had gathered nine points of the law to yourself. Your conduct of November last declared more forcibly than words the truth of the matter; there exists summits of authority at which the law is irrelevant. And indeed your assumption is correct. Our judge conceded as much during the Catonsville trial. He granted that no American President could be summoned to his court on charges of waging a war in violation of the Constitution. You stand, evidently, in the aura of that same exalted immunity.

Still, I think, in the errant way of a prisoner, such an arrangement should not go unchallenged. The law of the land must apply in principle to every citizen; otherwise the law is void in principle, and guilt becomes a matter of the spleen or caprice of those in power. No; if a priest is answerable before the law, so must a President be, or the chief of the FBI.

Therefore, I must state that you are guilty of a serious offense against the law and that I should invite you to undergo a period of rehabilitation, even as I am undergoing it. My reflections proceed carefully, and I hope with compassion. You are an old man, aged as several prisoners here, who languish and mourn at Danbury, while health and spirit fail them. I would not have you condemned to the fate to which you (and others) have consigned them—not even in my own mind.

Other alternatives occurred to me. Perhaps you should be invited to pass a period of time living among Black Americans. You held their martyred leader, Martin King, in peculiar regard. Perhaps the spirit of his people, their courage and patience, the poverty in which the majority of them live and die, their faith in human goodness, might revive you. Perhaps they could be persuaded to receive you into their midst for a time, as one more white man in search of a soul.

You might be brought to tears and a change of heart. Among these people, steeped in the wisdom of suffering, such things are held possible. You could share their buffets and humiliation as they seek justice in our courts, or healing in public hospitals, or survival on public welfare. The teeth of rodents, the cries of hungry children, might pierce the tranquil armor of your isolation and open you to the realities of life as experienced by so many today.

A like plan might be workable among our Spanish peoples, concerning whom you have vented certain feelings of late. Or among peoples of Appalachia or the slums of Brooklyn or Chicago.

But still, I think in near despair, who am I to choose for you, or for the peoples of poverty, the form of your soul's rebuilding? The people must choose; you must choose for yourself. No one can easily enter, as a friend or disciple, among those he has stigmatized. Nor can I choose, for you, so to enter. It might even happen that such despair, such anguish (as well as such invincible love and long sufferance and courage) as is the daily portion and resource of these people, would break you in pieces, as it nearly breaks me, each day I live among them in prison.

No, in the cold daylight of America, it is clear that my reflections are nearly hopeless. I cannot choose for you, or for the people, the form of your healing.

Still, perhaps my words have not been entirely without point. I have insisted, and continue to insist, that you stand under the law, in spite of all. You stand there, as I stand there. The government has obligingly set the term and condition of my punishment. If I refuse to apply the same harsh word to you, or to "punish" you even in my thoughts, it is because I continue to take seriously one truth—that no one can be punished into moral adulthood. Neither you nor I nor the prisoners in domestic tombs nor those in foreign tiger cages. No, if some, suffering the rigor of the law, choose to become human, which is to say, if they persevere in nonviolence toward the keepers of tombs and tigers, it is not because punishment or cages, or tombs, are tools of human change.

Such are reborn because they choose to punish no one, to work no violence in return for violence. Thus, they choose, when humanity is defaced by official violence, by war, by law and order masking lawlessness and disorder—they choose to love. In that choice, you are included. In that choice I venture to say, you will be saved.

For both of us, and for many others as well, whatever their circumstances of power or powerlessness, one question remains. It takes many forms; it is one. How shall we become human? How shall we live with others? How shall we so live that no one need die—whether of hunger, of violence, of vengeance, of despair, of the accumulated burdens of life, its injustice and poverty pressing him into the earth before his time? What law shall we keep so that no life be lost in the keeping? And inevitably, when is violation of the laws a vindication of human life?

In court, in prison, at prayer, I have come on only the most tentative answers to these questions. I can only say to you, I have come on the questions.

But I have never heard that, in almost fifty years of voluminous public utterance, you have framed a single such question. You have summoned Americans to many a crusade—against violators of law, against delinquents and deviants. But have you ever given thought to the victims, to the poor, to those who seek a life worthy of human beings, to those whose "criminality" is a great cry against injustice, against the law inequably applied, against institutional disorder?

This letter is a long one. I hope it proves neither burdensome nor accusative. I hope through it to offer you thoughts which are of more profit to you than the encomia of those who praise thoughtlessly.

My father, who died at 91, would say; a late wisdom is better than no wisdom at all. I pray for you, as for myself, that better wisdom.

Sincerely,

Daniel Berrigan, S.J.

5. LETTER TO THE YOUNG JESUITS

St. Ignatius Day, 1971

Dear Brothers beyond the wall:

I am setting down a rather rambling newsletter to greet you on St. Ignatius day. Also to thank you in the name of many brothers in prison for the stand you have taken against the draft.

Thanks are certainly in order. On reflection, nothing could be more fitting than that men of peace express their abomination of a free-fodder system that processes the living for death.

Let me, however, suggest a caveat. Your action is late. It was delayed undoubtedly by the deferment offered the churches by the state—an arrangement whose consequence is a deferred development of awareness. A tardy act on behalf of life is certainly better than none. At the same time, one is humbled by the reflection that others have gone further and faster to the heart of the matter (resistance) and have paid a far more grievous price than we clerics.

Further, an action of this type is self-defeating unless it opens you to the possibility of further resistance. It would I think be tragic if you declared your independence of empire, only to return home, confident that you had done your thing. Home to what? one asks. Institutions as usual, church as usual, Jesuits as usual? The poor of your cities neglected as usual, racism as usual, fail-safe war as usual? I suggest your draft statement has only started something you are honor-bound to pursue; either that, or you have started nothing at all, in which case your own sense of honor is surely in question.

Let me quite simply share my views in regard to resistance. Resistance to the war-ridden, blood-shot state is the form that human life is called to assume today. It is also the simplest, most logical way of translating the gospel into an argot that will be exact and imaginative at once. It is an occasion of rebirth, and a bloody one. It is also a choice. We will either die in our old skins (with all that implies of violated promise, personal despair) or we will come to second birth by giving our lives for others. (I plead guilty here to a fundamentalism that prison tends to hasten.) One gets reborn by saying "*No*" to the state—a "*No*" loud and clear enough to be heard, to trouble Leviathan.

We are required, Camus says somewhere, to be neither victim nor executioner. To be what, then? The alternative is the nub of the matter. Somewhere in the bowels of the state, or the bowels of the church, is the new birth gestating? One who will neither kill as required by good citizenship, nor be victimized by cowardice, silence, slavish obedience, cultural me-too-ism? Surely God and ourselves long for such a one to get born.

The new man or the new woman will certainly not be the product of spontaneous generation; born of our fevered and impure blood, an act of God—but just as certainly an act of ourselves. I assure you such men and women are coming to birth daily in prison. A helping word, a constant word of truth, an unselfish will to live for others—these bring us to birth.

I pray such a one is being born among you, too. No one else can respond to the staggering, life-and-death character of our needs today. You know these needs as well as I. You know too that the old comfortable arrangements between church and state are helpless to generate newness. To the contrary, they prolong the stereotyped, lethal "solutions" of war, racism, poverty.

And in proportion as we envision a life based on such arrangements, or benefit because of them, I think we dishonor Christ. More, we join in principle the destructive conspiracy which from Pakistan to My Lai to the Pentagon Papers is showing its hand as the American way of death.

The peace of Christ, it goes without saying, is not won by such complicity. That way of peace is something else; necessarily a humiliated *via crucis* today—no less than in the year of our Lord. It requires that our lives lie open to the fiercest winds of change, that we confront together our fears, our despair and dread of life, that we resolve to renew ourselves each day in fraternities whose only charter is the gospel.

Prison is one such way. I am convinced it is one that will grow in likelihood and import for many. More and more, work for peace is being stigmatized in America as criminal activity. More and more Christians are being summoned before grand juries, and given the absurd choice of betraying their friends or going to jail. Necessarily and with great moral courage, they are facing the simple likelihood of being locked up.

My brother has served two years in prison, myself one. We have won a place of trust in the lives of many other prisoners, especially the young. Our regime is a simple one; we read and study and work and discuss together; we also endure the oppressive and sterile prison atmosphere, with what grace and good humor we can summon. The experience is salutary—for me, in spite of everything; it is a privilege I could not have dared count on even a few years ago, something like landing in the uncharted other side of the moon. We taste powerlessness to the dregs, we know the capriciousness and cruelty of those who "do their job" to the hilt, grinding others under. Orwell's Newspeak is the real handbook in vogue; for rehabilitation read spiritual destruction, for religion read connivance with the police mind, for compassion read tortuous delay of justice.

Here, one survives in either of two ways. He accepts his definition as a loser who may now improve his score by becoming an idler, a loner, an informer. Or he takes his powerlessness as a cue to create new forms of power, within and around him; keeping his mind alert to oppose injustice, confronting his own cowardice and that of others with the example of great prisoners—Socrates, Jesus, Paul, Gandhi, Bonhoeffer, Cleaver. Taking the worst in stride, the atmosphere charged with threats of violence, intrigue, despair; descending into hell. At the mercy of an authority validated only by the clank of weaponry and a profound contempt for goodness. Realizing a prisoner is supposed to pay, day after day, a tribute to the power of death in this world. Refusing to pay, to submit, to go under. And yet, consenting to enter the *silva oscura*, a womb from which life, hope, decency might issue.

So Philip and I live; we work and pray, undergo bad days and good. We fail in charity and patience; and try again. We taste on our tongues the fate of prisoners, a taste both poisonous and healing. We wake in the morning; the first thought in our minds, like a needle in the flesh, is that we are in prison. Lights go out at night, the doors clang shut, we lie in the law's power, its hand closes like a fist. All day the guards, the blare of loudspeakers, the affront of being numbered and counted like cattle—these rub like a salt in the exposed tissue; a sardonic commentary on the land of the free. What rhyme or reason can there be in a system which is in principle antihuman, irrational?

There is none. You smile and guard your smile, a pearl of great price. Or you go mad.

Merton said somewhere that if we perish, we will go down, not at the hands of madmen, but of cold war functionaries, certified sane, Eichmanns with fingers on the button. I am inclined to agree. I am inclined also to reflect on the perennial sanity commended by the gospel and Paul, the folly of the cross. Certainly we have had enough, until it sticks in the throat, of the sanity of powerful rakes whose progress is recorded in the Pentagon Papers.

What of this other sanity, verified in Christ, in the saints, verified once more in our lifetime? It intoxicates one to think of it—the continuity, the universalizing of conscience, the conduct of war resisters today. You must be as grateful as I am, seeing the Acts of our Good Years enacted again. Who would have dreamed a few staid years ago, that priests and nuns would be taken in the common dragnet, would refuse to betray others, would display an unnerving cool in the face of Big Huff and Puff?

The great return to roots has begun. You and I have seen only the beginning, only the first act. But even that beginning is enough to get the blood racing with exultation. Christians in America have struck free. We could once be counted on by Caesar—for the silence that kills, for bargains arrived at across the bodies of the victims, for a blessing on violence and a sanction on murder. No more of that.

We must be clearheaded about the price of sanity. I mean by "the price" something quite concrete, as the authorities have already spelled it out to some of us. The price is refusal and resistance. If Caesar would make of the nation an abattoir, we refuse to be his executioners, his tourists, his do-gooders, his freeloaders. As Jesuits we will disrupt the business of death as usual; in our own communities we will perhaps eventually stop playing our nuanced dance of the mind, whose tune is beautiful and seductive, but for which someone must pay—inevitably someone other than ourselves. We will stop making liturgy an excuse for inaction, the life of the mind a cul-de-sac, our communities a compound for cultural Brahmins.

Caesar is fed up with some of us; he is even, now and again, afraid of us. It is good that he should fear us: fear makes his hand unsteady. The fear that afflicts the great saves lives—at least some lives. And the saving of lives is, I take it, our business, even to the point of laying down our own.

I don't want to sound gnomic or occult here. If I have any regrets about the past years, they center around the tardiness with which I went to Catonsville. If I had gone sooner, if I had had the gift of drawing other Jesuits with me, if a thousand Jesuits had come to their own Catonsville—and stood up to the law and the courts—what an effect we would have had, what horrors might have been averted!

But nothing of this happened. I was long bemused by a "normalcy" that blinded my eyes. I had been equipped to deal only with normal times; beyond lay an abstract no man's, no god's land—a war like every previous war, a war my church approved, a war against which no sanction was involved, since it was an American war, and we were Americans.

The war was at worst a discomfiting episode. Normalcy was still possible; we would invoke normal good sense, expect it of our military and political leaders; bless those who were unlucky enough to be shipped off, regret the inevitable deaths. Who was to foresee that so small a cloud would shortly cover the sky, that a sinister and terrifying plague was even then incubating, that moral disaster, assassinations, large-scale murder of the innocent, deception in high places, idolatry of violence would become the simple order of the day?

We did not foresee it, most of us. But we have seen it come to pass, a consumerism gone mad, making dead meat of men. We have seen human life cheapened to a disposable commodity, the war secretly extended, borders violated, words belie their murderous intention—all in the face of an unprecedented international revulsion.

You have reacted to these horrors, and courageously. Still I return to an earlier point. The human meat is still up for sale on the world market. Meat of women and children, of people in churches, in hospitals, in fields and factories. We are speaking of modern war, which makes of the most innocent, sacred, or banal activities a battlefield, a field of death. No one may plead exemption, no hearing for sex, age, condition, occupation. All are combatants, and so suspect, and legitimately objects of death.

In this sense, it seems to me, victim and executioner tend to blur in the minds of those who wage war, or expand war. It is not enough to play the executioner; one sees his opposite number in the milky eyes of children, and makes meat of them, too: mincemeat.

Thus the number of victims grows, along with the number of executioners (as we are learning). And in measure, the number of resisters as well—our hope.

Can you see your recent act then as part of a process, the other, far end of which you leave open? So many cannot bear to look on things in this way. As the war revs up (war can only rev up) they steel themselves for one moment, one act, one word—after which they fall back or disappear. They burn out, they cannot take the fact that life itself is a revolution, a series of deaths and rebirths, a passage from death to further life.

I am trying to suggest that the joining of issue between your peaceableness and the warmaking state has not yet occurred. The war needs the church, amnesiac, petrified; if not preaching a crusade, at least silent about murder. Such a peace requires of course great skill in dealing with dissent—not pushing too hard, overlooking the deviants when necessary. Up to now, the tactic is generally quite successful—how else could the courts sentence my brother to six years, Joe Mulligan to five, refuse us parole—except it sensed that church resistance was the business of a small minority (over whom Catholics would bicker bitterly) who could be considered, by the church itself, as deviants from business as usual? Your act will not be prosecuted; nor is it likely you will be summoned to a grand jury, given the fact of clerical exemption, and the disproportionate trouble that might arise from persecution.

So the question I suggest: Where do you go from here? We tried to offer one direction at Catonsville. We wished to declare an end to the era of good feeling between our church and the warmaking state. And since we had no power to promulgate such views (those in authority were quite content with the flourishing state of the alliance) we took the matter into our own hands. We invaded the Sanctuary of Caesar, dragged out his paper idols, and burned them to ashes.

Fire and ice. Play with fire, land on ice. There were no exemptions from that law, even for clerics. Rejoice with us. We have won our point; the era of good feeling is over. The government is furious with priests and nuns. It finds us "a serious danger to the security of the United States." Such was the judgment, straight-faced, of the Department of Justice in its effort to jail a nun recently.

So great a power, quaking in its boots before so few? Neither guns nor blockbusters, nor antipersonnel weaponry nor contingency plans, nor Vietnamization, nor tiger cages, nor Song My, nor public lies—only a few Christians, nonviolent in principle, fed up with bad news, striving to create in their own lives good news for others—the formula is very old, it might work once more. In any case, we tried.

To bring these notes up to date I want to share two recent events with you.

In June of this year, I nearly died in prison. During a routine trip to the dentist, I underwent a "massive allergic shock" after an injection of pain killer. For several hours I struggled to breathe, in and out of consciousness. A heart specialist downtown later told me that, apart from the skill and speed of the prison doctor and several inmate aides, I would certainly have died.

Prosit. Off and on as I struggled for breath, I recalled a certain bargain struck at Catonsville. We had put our lives where our words were. And God was a curious being—He might at some point decide the pledge had come due. Here and now, I thought—maybe in prison.

We had lived with death for a long time. It made of the last decade a bloody passion play, in which spectators barely survived. Vietnam, Biafra, assassinations at home, now Pakistan. David Darst had died by fire, Merton by mischance, lately the brother of Eqbal (defendant at Harrisburg) by a fall. The deaths of our friends had about them an absurd aura, almost a quality of play, as though God were testing our sense of the ironic, our sense of humor, along with our capacity to take the tragic in stride. Could we deal with death up close (as we claimed we could)—close as our own brothers and sisters, close perhaps as our own bodies? And could we accept it when its guise was not particularly noble, heroic, mythic, but banal, chancy—a bad electric circuit, a car out of control, a plunge off a bridge, an innocent needle?

Another episode. In late July the parole board met in D.C. on Philip's and my application. As you know, we were turned down cold. In Philip's case the decision was one more in a long series, each of them designed to keep indefinitely out of circulation the

First Nonviolent Troublemaking Cleric of them all. In my case, there was a different twist. Two MD's submitted evidence on the near catastrophe of June and the general worsening of my health in prison. No go. The evidence was ignored, in view of the nefarious character in question.

But suppose we had been paroled? I confess I would have left prison with a curious sense of uncompleted work, a sense almost that something had gone awry. Parole might have been one instance of official compassion, but what of general official savagery, what of the war? Why indeed should I be treated differently from a prisoner in the Vietnam tiger cages, or a prisoner in the New York Tombs? There was indeed a strange kind of relief implicit in learning the decision, once made. A notoriously repressive government had made a decision that deserved the name "radical." No concessions to lawbreaking priests. So be it.

Brothers, I must share with you my unease, as I ponder this letter. Unease about the Society, the church, about my ability to act as your brother, about my language; unease, I suppose, about my life itself. Can I speak of a few of these, clumsily and tentatively?

The prison experience, a kind of harrowing of hell, also plows up one's own existence, his attitudes, his imagination, his use of language. His attitudes: Am I a believing man? His vocabulary: What words does a believer use in addressing his brothers from prison?

On the one hand, one is reluctant to use "religious" terms; he grows sensitive to the bowdlerizing and bastardizing of religion in the service of oppression. We, too, have our chaplain, a captive of Caesar; more often than not, we have been judged, manacled, strip searched, our mail censored, our visits spied on—by religious men, good Germans "doing their jobs," good Catholics.

Yet I must also say something of the religious character of life here. Solitude, the presence of suffering, the breaking of men, the need and opportunity for prayer, these make one's faith more acute. I believe in Jesus Christ. He sustains my spirit, he speaks to me in my brothers and sisters. I reflect upon the hours when I lay close to death, and I confess to naïve surprise that I did not see His face. I saw only the faces of Philip, of the doctor, of my fellow prisoners, sober with grief and shock. Were their faces the forms of His own? I do not doubt it.

There is another dialectic to things. Dying in prison, or living there, is from another point of view completely secular in character. Even at the point of death, I was not in any sense consoled, I had to struggle to remember that it was probably important to pray. It was as nearly impossible to pray as it was to breathe, a moving of mountains, a Sisyphus work of faith. God did not show his hand—or his face. Dying was a kind of banal continuum with living—crowded, messy, gray, noisy, a limbo by day or night. The senses are toned down, the body and mind tend to lassitude, the sweet stimulus and variety of the world are a forbidden fruit, a remembrance of aching grief. The outside world visits us, under strict supervision, as though we were terminal patients or mental defectives. The place is something like a Jansenist novitiate set up in opposition to the worst of all possible worlds—except that with us it is the world that must be protected against its own offscourings.

Too evil to be borne, or too virtuous to mix; in any case, locked up. It is the image of lockup (what stays in, what stays out) that strikes me as a way of expressing the secular "taste" life carries here—unmistakable as brimstone on the tongue. We are locked up, a way of dramatizing the deep mystery of evil—are in purgatory for the accumulation of merit in Caesar's eyes, doing time in the pit, the languishing and labor that precede redemption. With this crucial difference—the human shape of God's love is absent, the search for ways of change, in life and society, the means to make us conscious, politically literate, alive to our world. No one in authority gives a literal damn; they are here to see that no inmate dare do so. The goodness implied in divine caring, responding to, prevenient to human goodness is excluded by law.

This means something quite simple and concrete, as far as prison discipline is concerned. Everything that touches on the life of prisoners must be literally second rate; as in hell. The quality of what is quaintly called "custodial care" is second rate (though it absorbs some 95 percent of the budget, a pretty exact application of national values, national military spending). Food, religion, books, programs, edicts—all are dog-eared, outdated, tepid.

Nothing in prison corresponds to a deeply felt gravitational pull toward excellence that in the world outside, in the Society, existed at least at the edge of life, a gnawing in us, a call to us; the perfect sacramental mysteries, the homilies and texts, the demands made on our lives, prayer, chastity, the clear and consistent structure of a life the saints had lived, and we were invited to live. Nothing of this here; not even a show of some sort of desacralized humanism. We wear old army clothes, eat mediocre food with half an appetite, are cheated at the company store, defrauded in sweat shops putting together weaponry against Vietnamese. We listen to windjammers instructing us in law and order, are presumed to be as infantile and incoherent as our keepers, are ordered about in a cynical dumb show. The absence of ideas, alienation from nature, suppression of instinct, the presence of fear, the itch of violence—these are the ingredients of an ideological secularism, drawing on the dregs of bad religion, jingoism, despair of human nature.

Still we try to deal with this—because we believe, at the edge of unbelief. The absence of God is indeed a triumph of the state—but I reflect that, with a crude but altogether sound logic, Caesar may have created a situation in which faith comes into its own. He has nearly quenched the light. Does he serve to thrust us into the dark night, which is the proper atmosphere of faith? I believe the worst he can do is the prelude to the best which God will do. It may be that the lord of this world is already reduced to a slave's rule—dealing death to all that is parasitic and moribund in us. If we are hopeful, patient, modest, inventive, and firm of heart, we will see great things. Even we.

Let me close with a few remarks on the Society.

Father General's visit was an occasion both of comfort and discomfort. On the other hand, he had come to the prison in spite of urgings from American authorities in Rome not to do so. I salute the good sense that ignored such rude effrontery. More, he brought to this unlikely place his personal charm and nobility of spirit—no small gifts in such a setting.

On the other hand, I looked in vain after his departure for some statement relative to the war, or to Jesuit resistance. There was none, to my knowledge. Evidently he had conceived his visit to me as a personal chore of charity; he visited prison as he would visit a hospital. The burning moral and political issues surrounding my incarceration, the opportunity to place his prestige in the service of peace, these were lost. He never took up in the course of his travels in America the questions I addressed to him some four years ago, after my return from Latin America. These questions are still to the point; they touch on the complicity of Jesuit institutions with the military establishment, in university research, chaplaincies in the armed services, presence of ROTC on campus, and Society investments.

I believe, therefore, and say it with regret, that his visit was an act of charity at the expense of justice; it expressed personal concern but ignored legitimate and urgent issues. It also tended to reduce me to an object of charity—even (as Jesuits have written) to an instance of the large-heartedness of the Society: Look, we put up even with Berrigan!

Such conduct is painful to me, but it is beside my present point. If indeed I am a cause of bitter division among Jesuits, it would seem sensible to pursue either of two courses: (1) Let me be dismissed from the society as a troublemaker, or (2) let the issues I have written and spoken and preached about for years, and which eventually brought me to prison, be taken up by Jesuits with the seriousness they warrant.

Meantime, I suggest we take seriously a solemn warning set down some years ago by Philip and recently echoed by Gordon Zahn. The American church is in a worse moral position before history than was the German church under Hitler. For German Catholics, access to information on the Jewish question was extremely hard to come by; today, the truth about Vietnam is out. Then, protest was forbidden under the heaviest penalties; today penalties, even for conscientious lawbreakers, are comparatively slight.

In the baleful light of the deaths of whole peoples, deliberately and repeatedly inflicted, our neglect of the moral questions raised by wars, our petty concerns about religious renewal, seem to me a blinding form of self-deception: good housekeeping in a plague-tormented city.

I must conclude that, for my part, to be a marginal Jesuit is a permanent state of life. I must draw from alienation the spiritual resources needed to persevere in my search for manhood, conscience, the will of Christ. Certainly I cannot be a Jesuit because I discover moral clairvoyance or heroism in its leadership. But my hope is strong that these qualities are emerging in a number of young Jesuits.

To all, the pledge I made a year ago still stands: I am at your side in the struggle; I ask you to stand at my side also.

Someday we will have our retreat together, and meditate and rejoice in our confessing brotherhood. Meantime, struggle. A world is possible in which the murder of children is not an acceptable "way of life."

My hand over the wall.

Daniel

6. FAMILY LETTERS

[The following letters were written by Daniel Berrigan to his mother, to his brother Jerome and sister-in-law Carol, and other members of his family.]

Danbury
10/12/70
Mon. P.M.

Dear Ones.

What you do for us here, heads & hearts! It was as usual a very pure kind of joy—and bracing too, when we saw you on the hillside. Then the children run down like healers in their own right! I was literally shocked to see how they had grown; mostly the changes in their faces, something I find beyond prediction. One grows so used to the faces of oldsters and tends to equate children's bones in somewhat a settled way. Well, they are more beautiful than ever—and so are yez, with your lamps within.

We will just have to take the ups & downs of this and that as they come. One is always chagrined when the smidgeons (sp?) allowed us are further hacked away, but what the hell, we've grown up on Clay Knoll and know what "making do" means. Dado would approve I feel sure, of the rigor and discipline of it all.

I suspect this is going to be a rich sort of year for all of us. When events so conspired, I tried to tell myself I saw so many priests sliding down the play yard on their pants into middle age. All major decisions made—nothing but a shabby decency at the end. And suddeny a great light shone—on us. Not that we saw it, but we believed. There was going to be a chance of second birth in middle age—an utterly new form of life, placed in other hands; a kind of second chance; out of which something might emerge for others, in a harried, bewildered time. Here we are. Even a promised land, if we can recognize the promise.

You were "into" this as you had been in everything. I almost said, a part of this—except that spiritual realities have nothing to do with parts and portions. You were wholly in this with the wholeness which love both demands & confers—whole loaf, multiplied, for all. This is I think a clue to the special joy, the "terrible beauty" which is born in our faces when we meet & part. When we scan each other, as though our faces were a topography of the weather of the heart—what is being born, what is dying, what we can bear together.

Then one thinks of our brothers and sisters across the world (especially of others here) and knows that on the common scale of mankind, we are being asked to bear only what good men and women are bearing everywhere—and much less than most. But enough, for suffering, for acceptance.

This is to say thank you for coming, for all the miles, for the good news, the children, for mamma, for it all. We go back and pick things up with more will. The hours weigh less.

Philip is well, I think patience comes harder to him, maybe because I expect less and ride with more, in the agony of change busting at the seams, change forbidden. We keep learning about one another, not having been (strangely enough) in such close conjunction for a long time. I tried to urge Betty to have his editor Joe Cunneen show "a little interest" by a letter or a report. Maybe you could second this. I have sinking moments when I reflect that his superb book has gotten so little appreciation.

Hope all was super at the Mayer's house. They are such a big part of our lives!

Safe home. I envision a good week underway for you all. We had Mass today. You were there.

 Daniel

Did you get to see Levine's drawing in the *N.Y. Review?* It went the rounds here. People found it hilarious.

Nov. 10, 1970
Mon. P.M.
Danbury

I thought I should follow Jerry's instructions & clinch this one in time & space. A foggy, blowing night, a holiday tomorrow, a good November under way. The passage of time brings healing, as it brings news, friends, the unexpected, the opportunity. Your visits always leave me younger. I can hail back to beginnings & recognize the stone in the throat—a young man's reaction too, way back to St. Andrew & early *mal du pays* as the French say, connecting it with a homeland & the malaise of ache that comes of distance from only a few faces, maybe one house, wherever the soul longs to dwell. Well, I follow you in the miles back, mostly praying for safe arrival, not to excessive weariness. The children are another ingredient in the great recognition scene; thank you for them as well!

Eqbal was here, finally and warmly—yesterday. What a surprise! he had come on from N.Y. all in a turtleneck sweater that looked like woven maple leaves in autumn. He was weary I thought, the national mood is not easy on good men—but radiant as well. We made the most of 2 hours & he went his way & I mine; good but good . . . Today. Paul M. came nosing through the heavy fog, arrived at 3:30 so we had to stutter along & try to make something of not much. He seemed pushed hard, parents a heavy concern, teaching, etc., etc. But the main thing, he got here & we both got to see him.

It looks as though we will both take the plunge into teaching next week, spent the PM trying to iron out things, get book orders out, etc. There is good cooperation from education dep't, they seem anxious to put us to the lathe. You will have to breathe heavy so that some ancient Barrigan Blarney surface again & make something of this essay, which I think can be so fruitful here, if all goes well. Will we ever be done with teaching? It seems to be a bubble in the bloodstream, a disease, but benign. Hope with us.

Now if Jeremy makes it, we can wind up this months time & go chasing the phantom turkey.

All sorts of people send books. The French psalms arrived from the Provincial. What a breath out of the past! I remember carrying the same paperback edition around France & elsewhere in '64 & then N.Y. in the years following.

Good letters from all compass points continue to hearten.

A friend discovered Robinson Jeffers & E. Dickinson in old editions in the library. Years since I looked at either. Pop was right, we're geese walking on noble graves.

Enuf nunsense. Love goes without saying—& gratitude.

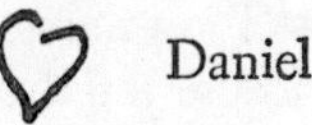 Daniel

Friday night
January 15, 1971

Dearest Mama,

A very short note, really nothing at all in comparison with all the thought and love which have gone out from here in your direction since you went to hospital. I am sure Jerry and Carol let you know of my phone call; it was such a reassurance. We got their telegram also, but *after* the phone call; these things have a way of being tardy as horses and buggeys (buggies?) these days.

Well by all reports the worst is over for you and you will soon be doing minuets with the grandchildren at Maywood and in the front lobby of Loretto Rest. Thank God. One cannot think of you except dancing, at least in your heart—and most of all on days when one wouldn't think it easy, or much feel like doing it. Days like the present, for instance.

Jerry and Carol's visit was a heart-lift; you will have heard Mr. Goodell was here the same PM; luckily he and cohorts had the good sense to clear out gracefully and leave us to our dear ones, their news of you, etc.

Then the lawyers came, including the rambunctious and cheerful

Mr. Kunstler, and my dear fellow Jesuit Bill Cunningham. And Tom Buck, with Congressman Anderson's regrets. All in all, a good week. Bill goes back for spring semester teaching assignment at Loyola U. of Chicago, so it was a kind of farewell in his case—a dear man and faithful friend.

We both remain cheerful in the present turmoil. I think we have a pretty strong faith to keep us humming—that is your due. We also have a sense that our present distress is acceptable to the Lord in behalf of many others who endure so much more than we; beginning indeed with the Lord and His mother, and not forgetting the saints. And your life has not been exactly a picnic, and you kept cheerful and worked hard for others through it all. I guess I am trying once again clumsily to thank you—as well as to assure you that in essentials we stand as well as we can, where we have always stood.

Well enough of that. We are being remarkably favored by the winter, it seems scarcely a dent in the late autumn weather, but not much snow at all; some cold but quite clear and bracing. And then today, a thaw such as Robert Frost wrote of, as a staple of Vermont winter. Deceptive, because it sets one's thoughts ahead to March and even April—and of course the worst storms can still be expected through February.

Anyway it is so good to get air and exercise each day—and to hope you may soon be able to do some walking—maybe in another month or so.

Our loving gratitude to all who are so kind to you in the hospital—the nurses and doctor. And to the Sisters at Loretto Rest, of course.

Now please write us a note in your own hand when you can manage. So we will know your recovery is complete!

Much love dear and daily remembrance at prayer—and at Eucharist

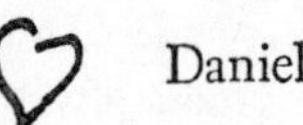

Daniel

I will send this to Maywood, not sure when you go home from hospital.

Fri. PM
Feb. 5, 1971
Danbury

Dear Ones—

Yr. wheels have not spun westward yet to the big tent site of frozen minihaha, and lo! I address these winged words to you. What a summer you make of our scene! I think the most we can do is exactly what we are doing—living through such hours and days with a certain wry good humor, taking the horror for the inflated paper dragon it is, being sun and air to one another as Papa Pollution huffs and puffs.

We have our own equipment and plan and idea of humans. It comes across, all of it, from the eyes, when we meet, and accounts for long silences, some laughter (saving!) and enduring connections that override the quaking hearts we all hold (one heart) in common, in our hands. Mom's heart, our friends; Phil's, mine; to what other hands shall we entrust those skinless beating organs of insight, second sight, even third and fourth sight, in weathers that would strike us blind, were we not clairvoyant by choice.

I chose all over again, when you come, to be where I am, to hate it less, to know it is right and just, availing to salvation. That, given me, is quite a choice, and has to be renewed often, and swallowed hard through the obstructed throat that rejects, if it were not aided by a vision, the meat of humanity. And then I try to choose for you too, because your lives like any good lives, are nudged by the times, to make a virtue of necessity. To the point where necessity itself loses its jagged outlines, like shrapnel or "antipersonnel" weaponry, and becomes the matter of choice. Freedom: to be set free, from the necessity of the flesh; comfort, good estate, an honorable name in the world, the rickety escalator upward, of church or state.

Every month you come, it seems a different figure has issued from the big town clock, declaring the hour. Usually a nightmare figure—we are supposed to be afraid, it is the first commandment of the times, if we take the common reading. The gargoyle, the warrior, the prince of the church, the guardian of locks and keys—they strike ominously, we are supposed to be figures of fear and trembling before powers too big for us, striking our doom, saying no to life, making beggars and robots and magic men of us.

I suppose a summons to a wedding is the antidote, the most unexpected thing! When the center is purportedly falling apart, two persons should calmly take one another, declare their love at the public hanging. So our friends have done; you might almost say *you* have given them the bad (good) example. If your marriage "works" (plays) when most things break down, there might be something to it for the rest of people.

That was why I thought we were really inundated with the news that came to us all in such a time—bemused, stricken to silence; finally perhaps in time, to be awakened to the uncanny, shattering rightness of such a happening. That two friends and so beloved of us as to be our other selves, should choose the world as we know they have chosen, and in virtue of such a choice, choose one another! The funeral (of the state) furnished forth the wedding feast. We shall never have done rejoicing and thanking God for another evidence of His hand, His heart, His "drawing" of man and woman to one another, to us, to Himself.

I hope tonight (you are at Francine's) is joyous, a recovery of breath, sharing, feasting, rest.

What shall separate us? When universal bad news is concocted to persuade us there is no good news left, a simple way opens; to *be* good news, to embody it, to smile it out, to make it available, in the gloom where death pretends, swaggers, claims, body counts; we have another way.

Be our dearest of heart, be yourselves.

When we see you, we see Mom, the children, all the families, the world. Who could ever pity us or call us deprived or indeed jailed?

Love to you and our thanks. Come again quickly: by that time there will be no more winter.

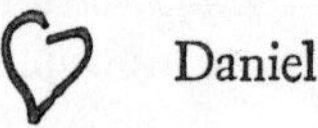
Daniel

Sunday, Mar. 20, 1971

)ear Ones—

News of Leland Hayward's death brought a sense of shock nd loss here. I had somehow not thought of him as such a 'heeler and entrepreneur so the *Times* obituary was quite a evelation. His beautiful spacious office on Madison Ave. seemed nore like a rich man's den cum memento room, quite warm nd cheerful, room for everything including as I recall a piano. remember when we first met he made no effort at any ort of come on or big time sales talk; he simply said he had een up all night reading the play and felt he had to do it and 'anted to talk about serious particulars—especially the crucial uestion of the best director possible. Peter Brook (*Midsummer Jight's Dream*) and Gordon Davidson were the first choices. Ve were very lucky, as things turned out. Leland was big and ttle, old hat and reborn all at one. He sent me to LA at his xpense to spend four days with Gordon and the troupe there ut added a small-minded note that I was to live inexpensively 'hile there (or refused to pay board and room, I forget which). n any case the I.H.M's put me up with pleasure at their ollege, I was never a Beverly Hills Hotel afficionado. T'was ever thus! He agreed I should get some notes down on the ackground, techniques, spirit of the play—and was, as I got econd hand, outraged because I wanted a certain space in 'hich actors could improvise and the audience be involved. So t went. This latter prospect as far as I know, was not realized.

He was shook by the new indictments and went about vondering what effect they would have on the play. Ha!

He came here once, and the visit was welcome and he amiable. don't remember that he was severely shaken by seeing his laywright on ice—but there was enough for both of us—& e kept his cool.

Like all the rich and great he had people about him to do lmost anything at a moment's notice, and he endured little f the dirt, grit and foulness of N.Y. slogging. But now and hen he would let out some sense of deep grief at family troubles; there was the glittering panache, and then the rut of existence, and the real was sometimes outdistanced by the apparent. I don't know what all this has to do with eternity. Apparently he suffered greatly in his last days, and knew he suffered. I hope the Lord turns him on.

Spring has turned on, to a degree, here. A beautiful tempestuous day with snow at morning and clear earth by noon. Sun and hard winds. We had some good paddle ball, and after this I will go & pray with the Quakers.

Many visitors this week: Paul O'Dwyer and Paul Mayer, Cunningham, Bender, Liz and the five, Francine, Kunstler. I think we are getting better at treading water together and taking turns on the life raft. No one has gone under, quite the contrary. Late this week there is a plan to bring the co-conspirators along; it will be good I think. I have never even met one of them. Stringfellow wants to join the lawyer team—a decision which means a great deal to all of us.

I don't know if you saw notice of Riemer's book, *The New Jesuits*. A copy came in here, it is a mixed interview bag, with many eels squirming about, a reflection of the times certainly. How unthinkable such a book would have been even ten years ago, and what a parody many earlier things—novitiate details, tactics of superiors—seem in the cold light of dawn!

Betty says Doubleday is going ahead with the Murray book. According to the *Times* (did you see Casey's piece on the editorial page Friday? hilarious) the paperback project with the H.C. *Quarterly* is also in the works. Through Jeremy we are trying to stop Nobile's two pieces from being included; but of course the decision is out of our hands.

The whole thing seems to me quite inflated and to that degree diseased. Like a huge vacuum in the media maw, elephantiasis in reverse. Sometimes I see how right old Picasso is, and want to lock up my goodies for 100 years or so. When we get bought or sold this way, one has a sense not only of spoliation and exploitation; but that people are making mud idols and transferring their personalities to them; alienation from responsibility and life. But maybe I'm just getting old here. You'll have to tell me. We would like to remain decent and modest in it all, and encourage people to find their way, which is by no means necessarily ours. What I object to is becoming the meat for a sacrificial feast.

Anyway today is Laetare Sunday and as usual I'm out of it. But not really. Enough joy comes through, from you, from dears and goods everywhere, to set winter off and make the streams flow. Thank you, you are in our hearts—

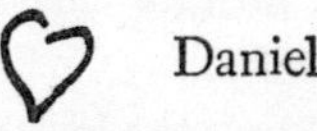 Daniel

Fri. night
21 May 1971

Dear Jerry and Carol.

I have some good notepaper w. a fish etc., but presently unavailable. I am in fact undergoing the tender mercies of Mother State in the hospital where I have been for two days. A damned uncomfortable kickup of the old ulcer laid me low. Imagine!

Lots of good care. Today Liz and Jogues and three priests came w. a copy of *Dark Night* and I spent an hour in their company, a tremendous BOON.

The Dr. had me on some dream stuff for a day. Today liquids and Maaaalox for coating of sed interior. Liquids and ice cream. I will be available for the fourth (wh. haven't checked but hope it is a Thursday and will include the next day too?).

Am overwhelmed w. everyone's goodness here; flowers, cards, visits. Now there is a BUBONIC PLAGUE KEEP OUT or some such sign on the door and things are quieter. The doc will come in esp. to see me Sat. and Sun.

Phil leaves Mon. AM for new arrangement in H'burg. He (and I) hopes to be back shortly. That doesn't make sense. He hopes and so do I.

We were angered and chagrined by LIFE to-do. Lawyers in their inimitable middling way, saw a real value in it: "things laid on lines." We who had suffered through much of it, thought of betrayals and blindness. To who we are and why, and from whence.

Someone found a passion flower out by the greenhouse and brought it in. It is so minute and waxen and geometric as to make me think of a plastic put-on. But in a bowl of water it is closing for the night: almost like an infant.

The news of Jerry's eye is so reassuring. I hope our next sight of him will see things entirely healed. My sole consolation is that all transpired in spring when teachers normally take such a beating, with papers and grades. This June he can just grin at it all.

News on the big fronts continues hot—to say the least. And there will be more, out of Pa. Those who are ready know their history—it's all happened before. So why (I ask myself) shock or dismay?

Mom wrote this week. I'll have to answer soon, but didn't want to hassle her with any news to be interpreted as bad. Everything's great, people couldn't be better.

Love,

Daniel

See yez soon.
!Big kiss all around from us!
Lew Cox wrote good long letter.

I get the greatest kick of being treated like a Dresden shepherdess. Chaplain, warden, caseworker; all in today. Could it be I'm all *that* loveable? Ha!

Graham Greene sent nice note and proofs of new book from Paris.

Monday and Tuesday
May 24, 25 1971

Dears,

Phil's sojourn should be ending today. I have no news beyond rumors, but since a rumor mill availeth nothing, I'll hold this through the P.M. news. If nothing of substance has happened, so be it.

Leonard Bernstein was here today. He seemed tired and

harassed but gentle as a lamb. He said the press has coined a new word, "Catholic Chic" to describe the meeting-party last wk, at which they raised 30 grand for the cause. He wants some help on a musical thing he's doing for opening of Kennedy Center in D.C. in September. I don't honestly know if I can be of any help but am willing to give it a try. In any case it was rewarding to be with such a good guy for an hour. He has some delightful theatre music going for the opening. I'm not at all convinced it needs any embellishment. But we'll see.

He seemed quite awed at the prison thing, etc. Almost like waiting in a novitiate or old time rectory. My own breeziness I hope helped lighten things to a degree.

By the way, feeling more and more chipper and shd. be getting out of the hospital tomorrow. One good sign is that it's getting to be a drag. The doc won't let me return to work until next Monday which I think is a good idea.

Good news also on Jerry's eye. As on Mom. Will you be able to come so as to stay overnight & have visits both days? Seems more humane to yrselves) & eminently more satisfactory!

One of the nuns this wk. had a copy of *Dark Night* book which I had not seen. Wanted Phil to get an early surprise copy but I guess it was not possible to leave it here. So it goes.

Many friends leave all the time. The place is like a squirrel cage when all is said.

P.M. Well I see there was no great news in Harrisburg so will expect Phil back maybe tomorrow and yrselves certainly next week.

Please don't do any worrying as I'm feeling absolutely first rate, and all is well here—

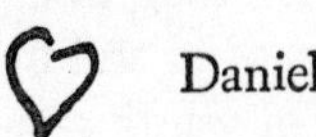 Daniel

*Sunday P.M.**
6/20/71

Dear Ones,

A note to say *especially* a Happy Birthday to Carol; I will be late by a couple of days but so what? The main thing is that in perilous times we are all still around to get and receive greetings. As well as to grow in the right direction, which is younger.

We have all sorts of good visitors and messages here—yesterday a young lawyer Charles Nesson from Harvard, and in P.M. Bill Stringfellow, a beautiful and instructive combo. Charlie has been in on the Harness-berg thing from the start but just got free to see us—perceptive fine young guy. Bill was as ever an understated joy: he has had a few bad days lately but shrugged them off as "normal." He was off to preach in Philadelphia.

I am back pushing the chow heavy and in general putting my money back in the World Bank after that impulsive near-withdrawal of 10 days ago. Whatever came over me! as Becky Sharp would say. In any case the "spell" (as one paper had it) is broken and I am planted ON (not in) terra firma firmly as a 10 foot clown. Sometimes it seems as though it was all fabricated by someone's (my own?) fervent imagination: but no. You were really there that day (and the week after), so was I. So were all those other worried uncertain people and in the midst I almost nudged into midstream. However. Restrained I wd. think, as much as by anything, by excessive love and longing and memories that cast me forward as well as back.

Jerry. I think your prayer to Merton got him into motion. At least the food thing seems fairly functional again, on thin eggs at times but still bringing on the older onrush of energy and a sense of wanting-to-be here, that marrow of will which the world both requires and bestows.

Well I prate on. The whole damn thing has been just short of ineffable. Youse came and saw and I recovered breath. Thank you. I had hoped to have a poem to send our dear girl, but nothing occurred. I am vain enough to think though that the happy outcome of last week's Peanut Pushing Party will compensate.

Much love, prayers, gratitude for your coming—and coming. We love you: O *adrenalin to the vertiginous ventricle!* (sp?)

I desist.

Mercifully.

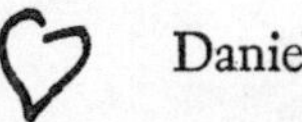 Daniel

* *The above letter was written as Daniel Berrigan was recovering from an allergic reaction to Novocaine which almost cost him his life.*

*Thurs., July 14, 1971**

Dears,

I didn't know if you would find the reverse funny or not. I hope so. Buck brought a Swedish poet & writer here from Block Island yesterday. A gentle good guy also carried a big daisy from the same real estate.

Leonard B. and Gordon refused visit. Too bad, I was hoping to hear some news East & West. They might try approach to congressman but don't know if they consider it that urgent.

Christina & Bridget wrote here and may make it, depending on the A.M. B.M. of the gods.

Lee Lockwood also was here. Seemed in good form and somewhat chastened and more thoughtful.

They decided it wasn't gout in the elbow but rheumatism and gave me a plunger of cortisone. Needles, ugh! Said elbow still in snit but change of heart expected.

Are you all thriving? Still redolent here with your visit which gives a big whirl to the wheel of fortune and lands on target. We win all the way. We both go before board Monday A.M. Let the Lord see to it.

Much love & brevity,

Daniel

* *The above letter was written at the time that Daniel and Philip Berrigan were to appear before the parole board. Parole was refused both of them.*

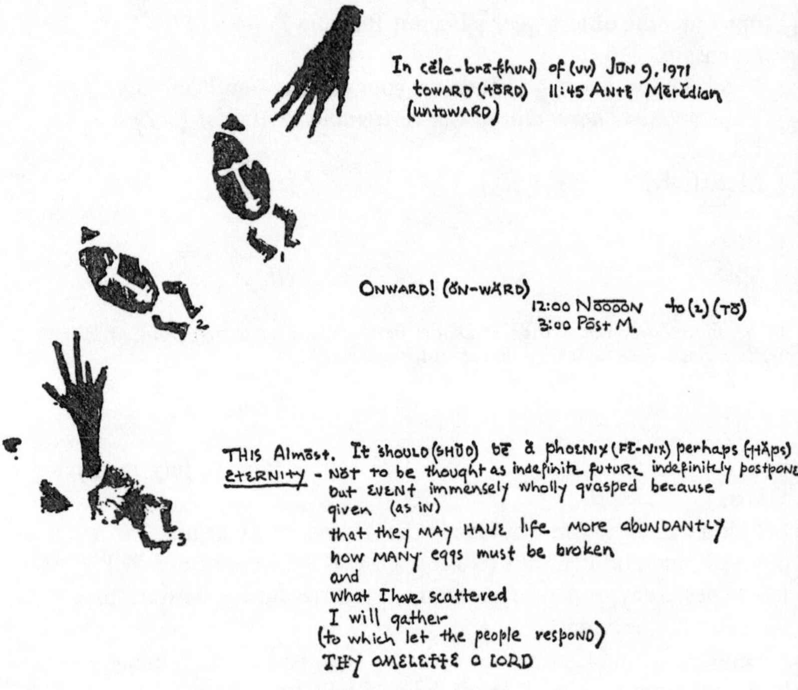

In cēle-brā-shun) of (uv) JUN 9, 1971
toWARD (tōRD) 11:45 ANTE Mērēdian
(untoWARD)
1
ONWARD! (ŏN-WĂRD)
12:00 NOOOON to (2) (TŌ)
3:00 Pōst M.
2
THIS Almōst. It should (SHŬD) bē ă phoenix (FĒ-NIX) perhaps (HĂPS)
ETERNITY - NOT to be thought as indefinite future indefinitely postponed
but EVENT immensely wholly grasped because
given (as in)
that they MAY HAVE life more abundantly
how MANY eggs must be broken
and
What I have scattered
I will gather
(to which let the people respond)
THY OMELETTE O LORD
3

Tuesday
8/10/71

Dear Jerry and Carol.

A note I'll begin today and even hopefully succeed in drawing to a close.

I am reading Bonhoeffer & the Marxists and am struck by certain similarities. It seems as tho both parties by their free acceptance of the preliminaries of the future, had indeed become parties to the future. The question both B. and Marx & Lenin were sweating over, was "What are we to build for the future?"

I realize more and more the serious and even unique form the question takes, especially since present forms of life and their structures seem guaranteed to preventing us from seeing any future at all.

Most people seem to quail before the question since it is outside their capacity to deal with. Because, simply, their moral environment does not favor the growth (force the growth?) of the New One.

On the other hand, what is under consideration is not simply another silly putty stereotype. Far from it. Yet this is the way the human future is often presented—a sanitized version of the dehumanized present, a decent cadaver granted a more pompous burial.

I think on the other hand, of something quite simple, a departure.

We have first of all certain classic hypotheses which ought by reason of the practical test of time, differing cultures etc., to be taken seriously.

Among these are the power and value of suffering.

I want to be political here, or practical, timely. All the great men seem to have gone through a knot hole phase. Not once, say, in their youth, but repeatedly. Cubits were added to their stature by the quite serious will and weaponry of those in power; to cut them down. They are then seen as survivors of a catastrophic period which they precipitated—and endured.

We are not to see them as victims. If the pathetic shines through it is because they came to a certain luminosity, a softness of depth instead of a mirror glare; but the flesh is always backed by bone.

In the case of most, mercy when they came to power proceeded from their prior subjection to merciless power. When they lapsed from this mercy, as each of the first generation Marxist leaders did to a horrifying degree, one can at least say his sins are known for sins, and repented of. No stains here, at least the moral norm allows one to speak of their honoring it, even by deviating from it, consciously.

The hypothesis of God. It has become almost an anti-hypothesis among Christians, even. The causes are fairly well known; social and racist and war copouts, mainly. And the subsequent ennui and even disaffection, the ills of the world transferred to the Creator. Simplicity of heart lost in a maze; to the point where His existence is pushed back to the roots of life, and squeezed out even at the roots. People are afraid or disgusted; He has failed them. And death has made such inroads into formerly healthy communities, whose members could not ride with a current that threatened unassailed secure areas. Terror takes over, and numbs the heart. It becomes scandalous to invoke a providence who is silent while the innocent go under.

It is necessary to invoke Him with the constancy and courage we once knew when all else seemed to fail us. Energy, will, the overflow that met the times, and coped. A new scene, a church that is a husk, a civil authority suddenly turned oppressor. The "necessity" is a cry, straight out of existence; it is necessary to exist as a believer, because to believe is to be human, and one will be nothing less—even in Dachau or in Danbury. "Not to deny in the darkness what we affirmed in the light."

What strikes me is not the chaos or discontinuity of the times, in comparison with what we literally "become used to." But their invincible continuity with real times, more generously understood. In such a view, we are not seeking, with all sorts of debased bargaining, to hang on to privileges, exemptions; but to stretch out to the universal in our time and every time. Thus to purify our understanding, not only of the common life here and now—but in every time and place. This living link is generally a missing one—it is engendered by what we used to call grace. Short of such a gift we are distracted of mind—deluded into thinking our sweet flesh bears the spiritual stigmata of others. Generally we are zombies, short of the inhabiting Spirit. Come then!

We need to be in the right place to call upon God. The gospel requires that we read it in something like the place, atmosphere, style, in which its words were first written/spoken. Short of this, all sorts of false reverberations are set up, delusions are drunk in like living water. Prison would seem by way of contrast, a good start. Or resistance as a style. We won't get far by way of a future until this is more generally recognized. Short of it, much bickering and bitterness and loss of time. And the invoking of God, not as Common Father and bestower of unity, but *parti pris*.

Wednesday

I had hoped to get this out to you yesterday but events have a way of catching up. I hope you are not seriously flapped by latest idiocy [the indictment of the Harrisburg Eight]. We shall have to see what develops, Anderson is due today. Jim, Rosalie, Anne, and Honey here yesterday, good hilarious visit.

Monday Night
8/16/71

Dears,

This thing (over) didn't quite come off, which is no wonder given the times and "faith and morals being exposed to so many and such violent temptations," as old B'more Cat #2 used to say so eloquently.

I wish I had some news but am empty as the Liberty Bell in a Republican year. Kunstler was here yesterday and Buck and Anderson Friday but these gentlemen had not been west. [Philip had been transferred to the Federal Prison Hospital at Springfield, Missouri.]

I am slowly bottling my fury and loneliness in expectation of a good vintage, eventually. I have seldom been so angry but of course the task is to make anger useful and thoughtful; I am trying. I remember writing of Phil once that he wasted no time licking his wounds. All such observations are helpful; and a source of rue, as they tend to come home to roost. There are several assorted claws in my shoulder right now.

Are you all well? Actually now & again we get an inkling of the common lot of prisoners. Then one thinks his whole life is being served in inklings, a little like Aunt Maggie's teaspoon doling (literally hard candy to "The Gang" on New Years' Day). That was to get us used to being deprived, and grateful to our betters for putting up with us and even now and then rounding off a corner for the infested, occasionally deserving poor. Such talk is still heard. But I feel caught betw. the teaspoon and the big ladle. We have some moral clout against Big Brute, but not much. Those of our station are not prisoners; prisoners are not of our station. Whom dare we speak for? Live for? Everything is approximate and to that extent damnably unsatisfactory. The most sensible thing being to swallow hard, squeeze a smile out of the damp shroud, and go on, meeting with what hands and the faces beyond, which darkness allows for. The practical intelligence, the well practiced heart. Or something.

We had a citizenry of utopia arising in the outer milder circle of hell itself—popsicle hell; peopled with heroes, friends, men.

Such rarity in the genenalized debased coinage of the black guarded pocket. All goodness was given freely, with the cheerful nobility that mocked the subalterns of the Mortuary. It was a little like the reasonably verified events of circa 30 A.D., a wandering Socratic rabbi and his ten or twelve friends, all of whom it is said lived good and made death good, as well.

Luv dears,

Daniel

Wed. August 25, 1971

Dear Jerry and Carol,

2 good letters from yez this P.M. With glowing words about Springfield, almost enough to make one feel a place of purgation is by no means a final option. It wd. be understating the case most limply to say I was thinking of you and of Philip all weekend. He remains so large a part of whatever life is allowed to beat here, the place seems to live on a kind of borrowed heartbeat after he left.

Did I write Cunningham and Bender were here yesterday? They are good men, trying to help keep the whole thing together and currently pursuing the health thing of which more later.

The Jackson horror grabs the vitals and closes on it. I wonder if the truth will ever be known. The positive hope is that the rotten shell of society will not indefinitely be able to contain the powerful juices fermenting even now, night and day, in the lockup vats. Of this too, society like it or not, more later. Of course in a popsicle jail one is spared the edge of the blade—so the life can be enervating in the extreme. The virtue of J. and Cleaver as well (I am convinced his prison years were the most authentic and fruitful so far) is that they put their necks to the edge of danger and dared death to possess them. Most prisoners are already resigned to death, which is to say, to prison; which is to say, they are already dead. I suspect this fierce young spirit will not easily die: it may even be that his end was a more useful and a noble one historically than Cleaver's alienation and violence by proxy. But we'll have to see.

Jack St. George was here for some 2 hrs. today. He looked in fairly good shape, though quite weary. He was given a medical OK in NY and went on to Chi to see his mother who had suffered another stroke. Also while he was in the US his father's last surviving brother, Jay, died in New Haven. I remember Jay and Mary his wife from old days—they came to hear me preach at Yale in the salad days of '69—an unexpected joy as I had not seen them in years. Anyway, Jack helped nurse his mother through her second stroke and then came back to NY; he leaves for Rome on Saturday. I found him perceptive and gentle as of yore, quite aware of our multifarious pestilences of spirit and scope, and yet serene as well. Was struck by his resemblance to his father, more pronounced than before—but where he comes by his temperament, out of Mrs. Fire and Mr. Ice, seems to me a kind of miracle in itself.

So we talked and talked, as though we were wandering about their old farm in the North country. It was restoring and meant the more because of long absence & present bars and Mars. So to speak. The Provincial of N.Y. is due here perhaps tomorrow. There will be a good deal to talk about when you come.

In a sense I grow quite detached over issues, results, etc. in what we are all undergoing—in our friends, brothers, our own souls. I feel more and more like a cretin when such ?? are in the air. The only point worth pondering I think is the fact that we are into life and death, willy nilly, up to our precious necks—and beyond. And thank God for it. There and I think nowhere else, free gestures are possible: one can act, undogged by outcome, timing, rightness. To the degree the act is free, it is cut free from false connections to achieve real ones. My reaction is unpolitical and profitless: I am driven to admiration, joy, tears of communion with such moral grandeur. I am stricken and healed to learn a brother has put his life in a breach where death threatened my own. Such a gesture seems to stop all machines and reach like a death stroke or an act of creation, to the base of the soul. Also I think such acts do not encourage looks back or forward—but a stillness that goes very deep. And this is why prison for all its cutthroat absurdity and drymouth sterility is a good place to launch such gestures, or to be the beneficiary of them; there are very few distractions, in those so disposed, to "right actions," as Socrates would define these.

Well I will push this in a bottle and cork it and cast it. May it be a new wine!

Love & gratitude,
Daniel

come you ascend
the LADDER
ALL sit DOWN
we were poor, poor po
poor POOR poor
when we came
to this world
through the poor
PLACE
where the BODY OF
water DRIED FOR
OUR PASSING

all come
4 TIMES
with your showers

DESCEND
to the BASE
OF the LADDER
&
StAND
still

all all come
all ASCEND all come IN ALL sit down

N.A. INDIAN
chant

Mon. Anniv. Delano Grape Strike
9/20/71
Sunday A.M.

Dears—

It just had to be your fate to get one of these popsicle art pieces, a dim thank you indeed for a great trip and visit. Tried to be at least somewhat conscious of you on the road last night, it must have been a long last haul for you. I am also going to try to get some light on the mixup on inside outside visit. We were fortunate it didn't grind more of our time away in the official hamburger blender.

Maybe, who knows, by next visit our brother will be in our midst. There was a letter for me yesterday as well. All of them continue in good spirits, putting on some weight, but unknowing (at least as of Tuesday 14) what their fate is to be. So we will sit tight and be comforted. They are in better hands (America has so many hands) than say, the Vietnamese people; there are eyes upon them and friends interested, and all that makes a difference. Phil by the way complains of lawyers and legislators. Especially from the latter; they have received so many promises and so little achievement, one is hard put to know how they retain any modicum of confidence in such creatures.

Being in a seed bed of the future—really enduring the weather, solitude, dark etc. rather than splitting mesself down the middle w. fantasies, vagrant hopes: I mean to apply all this to Phil & the others. It means precisely enduring the present, not being cribbed by it, seeking out those elements of hope that can be carried across into some better human clime. I have the affectionate impression that he and the others are doing this very well, very consistently. There are elements of dispersion and pressure in their situation which speak to me deeply of a literal biblical time when a mystery is almost palpable. I don't mean to be mystificating—there are elements of a very simple and direct providence in plucking a chosen remnant out of the undifferentiated stews of the world, turning up the steam, heating up the growth. We never know the other end—we can only guess and marvel at what glimpse we get of it.

I am reading Thompson's Vol II of R. Frost's life. It is less interesting than the first. Our hero, once arrived, allows his selfishness full play, makes like a venomous dog in a rich manger, and hucksters his wares freely and broadly—as though indeed he were not so sure of their worth: as indeed he was not. Once you see him developing, the future I'm now into has a kind of fatuous inevitable quality. Indeed the only interesting parts are those rare ones that tell something of how the marvelous middle-stage poetry got written. But what an unhappy, envious, eaten soul he was, & how he paid and his family, for ever encomium paid the "Great Man" with the soul of a louse. I'm going through it rapidly always marveling in an unwilling corner of me, at how such great poems got written, what a cagey, self-knowing, transmuting skill he had—to make of the worst suffering of the insect state, a good and great thing for others. Maybe the poetry was the literal salvation—the only way out of the shell. He was lucky to find that way and we are lucky as well!

Speaking of luck is to speak of me. And to say thank you once more, yet once more. Youse are the greatest, someday we'll all have a thousand hours really to do justice to the twister.

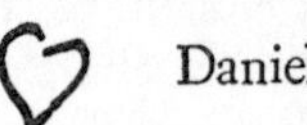
Daniel

10/1/71

Dears,

The fish is dismembered.

The eye is teary and sees the little man as headless.

In short a most discombobulated scene. Which says in effect how can you put art together when you never get a letter? (Well hardly ever.)

Phil is back over a week, we hope you had heard by now. We both wrote, among other ether waves that may have reached you. It is a good time for humans, in a closed circuit sort of way. That is to say, among large evils minor goods flourish like pearls or mushrooms in dark circumstances.

Our brother is thriving in his way, which is to induce thriving in others. So that altogether we make a creditable and gradual outgrowth.

2 dear old priest friends were here, first time ever, yesterday. Frs. Kohle and Murphy. It was quite like old times. We had often repaired in 64–6 to Grail country place in Cornwall N.Y. for Eucharist and self-cooked dinners and relief from Macadam Inc. This was not the same; but really the same after all.

The sun seems to be struggling through here, first time in memory almost. One almost feels at times as though he were keeping an Everest diary in a coal mine "If you get what I mean."

Much pondering and exploring of what lies (may lie) ahead. Presence of friends an unmitigated beatific joy. Vacuums filled, with ambrosia and lotus.

Lawyers have come and gone. If their attendance spells a criterion, we should shortly be among the most virtuous of men.

I am finishing Robert Frost and Martin Chuzzlewit. The former to wonder at in dark astonishment; the latter a taste of the insanity that induces health. Mrs. Gamp alone would supply a rich and ongoing model for a lifetime; My ideal of boozy virtue. We think of you all as schoolbooks open and young minds begin stretching out and out their spaces to the empyrean. There is perhaps no one of our literate majority of citizens who does not grind his molars in contemplation of daily lethal idiocies of power. Or (of same) who does not feel almost equally powerless, with us. In 10 or so years perhaps Mr. Professor Skinner of Harvard will have us transistorized into obedient odorless rodents under sedation, scurrying about a maze which has been made 2 make sense. Let us take advantage of the time remaining us—he seems to counsel—to be conscious and to suffer. And who will tell this comfortable tweedy destructor that he is, exactly, insane: but being in formation even though hopelessly off course, he has no one to break through? We shall have to, in small ways, ourselves. Well; this was not meant to be so sombre, all is really beautifully well here, as with furrowed brow and majestic beat we proceed to rehab the prefab.

You are in our hearts.

Daniel

Friday October 8, 1971

So you are there and we here, but as in every gift whether of flowers or friendship—each side aches with memory and is redolent with—what? Marigolds? Half was the surprise, half was the years, another half was contributed by the management, which is to say, the Grand Mongolian Plateau, crossing which makes a human being on the thin horizon, in the thin air, loom like an epiphany of 3 angels, at least! You see I make *three* halves of our visit, thus invoking the prodigality of truth, feeling, and the refusal of ripe and rosy melons to be subjected to body count. I suspect every life, once opened in taste & odor, wants to be a witness to such spiritual sur-plus as occurs to us when you came; as to you, we dream, when we come. Anyway. Here's to the three halves of the perfect whole which Plato dreamed and they tell me, Buckminster fools with. It is a structure (I invite) more rigorous than geometry and more exuberant than a rococco (sp?) ceiling, both bearing weight and rejoicing in weightlessness.

I hope you left reassured that you found us in good fettle making the most of meager days with richness of reach and spirit. And that the assorted and multiplying absurdities find in us a rich reserve of owl's hoots; unrancorous wisdom flung against the dog's incursions. (I have never yet heard of dogs trapping an owl, no?)

I think you had come on a good compromise to the professional and family obligations—in coming that is for the solid 12:30–4:00 session and thus to speak, resurrecting 2 birds with one stay. How! Remarkable how we were able to mingle delight with business and emerge as though twice born, the unifying ingredient being that deep secret elixir of the spirit. . . .

One year gone marks like a red X the transition, finally, from tourist to inmate—I mean as regards the soul, which cannot be hurried into a new shape or a new box but sticks out at the edges, even at the price of blood. . . . Now I say quite generally, I fit. Which I hasten to add does not mean one is institutionalized or pulled apart and remade like a junk collage; best to describe—something like seeing the thing from *within*, as though a potato grew eyes to see, instead of grafts. It sure is a damn potato world, the whole world, he wd. probably say esp. from Idaho or L. Island. I'm from Danbury; we spuds are mashed, deep fried, Frenchified, baked in kilns, planted in rows. We're working 4 potato power and have a Nat. promise from a big leader to wear a potato sack in our honor, and try a three legged race at the next Pratie Fair. Some hate us, some eat us raw. Shooting is damn poor cooking, our blood makes great vodka for file cabinet revolutionaries whose own blood makes good paint thinner. Anyway.

Please keep talking to Mom and getting good things for future memories.

Roddy's article for Oct 19 in *Look* is not at all putrid and has a few words about a few friends of yours.

Happy meetings with Jeremy.

Phil must have written our response to peace prize, a NAY cum regrets. I think this will make a good precedent all around.

Love dears and thanks and come back.

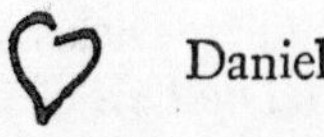

Daniel

Sunday night
11/14/71

Dears—

It's been a long time for which many apologies. Have received I think two of yrs. in past week, don't know quite how the times get to creep up and by so fast.

Not exactly a deluge of visitors so far this month. Betty came by earlier in the week; seemed in fairly good fettle in view of everything. She was sorry as ourselves about the mixup in Ithaca but I did my best with those troubled waters. I think if the Goldmans ever manage to get down here, we'll be able to make a new treaty. Did you see them lately? I thought I remembered a visit was on the books—?

Jeremy sent me the first copy of *Geography of Faith* which he had to go out and buy—a commentary of some sort I suppose on Authors and Publishers. I was intrigued by Coles' introduction which I had never seen; he reflects so painfully his own ups and downs with the course of things today. Of course several reactions to me were of interest since we never had much chance to collate or indeed to put things together after the short initial burst. Probably he felt some ground was too sensitive to tread on at the time. The whole fear of jail thing for instance was quite an eyebrow raiser. One never knows. Anyway Phil got the first copy and is now patiently going through it.

We had a visiting priest today. It was another rhythm, scarcely an improvement. One is struck over and over with the fact that jail thrusts in one's face—namely the necessity of going deeper on the religious question, of allowing the old (synod, bishops, etc.) to die in its own time, without undue stress or bewailing, meantime trying to live as though something else were possible or indeed attractive. What that is I suppose each of us is trying to live where we are, very much from day to day, hoping on in spite of all.

I am pretty well acclimated once more. It is an enormous help to have Philip back here. The defendants were with him on Friday, he seems fairly satisfied with progress, though it seems slow while the trial looms nearer.

Reading Dickens, James (*Religious Experience*) and a marvelous novel *The Last of the Just* by André Schwartz-Bart, from the French. Have you seen it?

A dear old Quaker lady who has written momma was here today for prayer. She told of a 200 yr. old tree in her yard which she calls Tree of Life and under which her grandchildren play. She is in her 70's and her *mother* just celebrated her 100 birthday.

Well that should wind up things for now. I hope you are having a taste of our peerless weather. We are so blessed, it is like a second autumn after first. Love to you all and our heart's best.

Daniel

Monday fore Thanksgiving
11/22/71

Dears, CHEERS!

The poor human is bandaged as to lips but the bird of paradise offers comfort—a kind of Thanksgiving theme. The Gibbons were here w. Quakers Sunday and Goldmans arrived unexpectedly on Friday. I was bowled over like ninepins, not expecting them until next week. It was a glorious time though very brief, they didn't get the word to me until 2:40 or so.

Other than that we've been infested w. lawyers. The most tolerable (understatement) being Bill S'fellow, who lent his benign straight play to us for an hour or so on Saturday. Phil and he had a fruitful xchange on coming events. We trust him because he's Xtian first and entrepreneur somewhere way back where it doesn't count or corrupt. Preprofessional in the sense of new testament about wh. most pros. couldn't qualify for nursery schule. Well.

Mama writes *great* letters, she keeps antennae out not only for the humorous and human where she lives, but also gives a good run down on children and parents and doin's at 106. You peoples keep her juices flowing like a maple in May. I think of her and forget the death dealers and wheelers: she don't die becuz she wants to live!

Well the Goldmans seemed in fine fettle, very little boy-oriented. I think. I was able to calm the waters on the ms difficulty though one never knows. In any case there was nothing to be gained by acting as though their project were still sensible or viable. We will help out on expenses, as I assured them.

Did I mention Bob Mitchell was here also, earlier in the week? Have still to hear results of his meeting with Bill C., latter was one lawyer who *didn't* show this weekend!

The remembrance Thursday brings a few clumsy inchoate thoughts. In my saner moments I see the good sense of isolating one feeling and thereby putting the world, one's life, circumstances, in a possibly new light. Do we not take even our own heartbeat for granted? Ordinarily for sure, until that long distance runner happens to miss an obstacle. . . . But in midst of many broken or buried lives and many more unawakened, and some consciously destructive and some few glorious with insight, verve and love—one pauses to think of his own heart—which labors on and turns labor to play because of those without whom it wd. shortly close up shop and hang out a "to let" sign. Never! You there—thank you! Things will grow worse, at least for awhile; I write this without knowing quite what it means, nor even wanting to; but knowing also that Harrass-berg awaits us all in the New Year. In that furnace the gold of those we love must be plunged once more, a further testing; not of soul, but of goodness. As the hideous Pretenders weave their web, we will have more reason than ever, I believe, to say thank you to God for one another "The net has fallen but we are free." Happy Thanksgiving.

Daniel

December 10, 1971
Merton

Dears,

A short one, at least to begin to say hello today. It really seems like *yesterday's* loss that took our friend away. [Gordon] Zahn tells in one of his introductions how that infamous retreat in early 60's started things off for most of us except of course vets like A.J. [Muste] who were already aged in the golden harness.

He [Thomas Merton] was surely one of those people you want everyone to know, like a sun god in the sun. Maybe that, the universal savor of true humanism—I can still taste our friendship on my tongue like a good communion and won't lose it until I trade it for his face.

He really did look like young Picasso and had brought along the sweaty climb all the funk and sweat of the flesh. He was still toward the end, bum enough to be able to give the bum's rush in his mind and tongue to all the bummers & phonies who haunt the cloister in the name of Dissolution. Funny how tricky & selective & right memory is, I can conjure up the day and hour at Lemon (Lemoyne) when I read his article on nuclear nonsense in the *Cath. Worker* and sat down to write him. He answered promptly why not come on down? I did and was hooked. O he was a reality sandwich all right. Driven 50 or so miles from the airport by bro. someone, blood brother of Brer Fox the abbot, hardly a word spoken all the way. Late supper and bedtime, no Merton, but a note to say he'd see me next day. Met him in AM under a big tree in the yard. He began to intrigue me w. his notion about man at the edge. He was still master of things and quite w. monastic events, as well as novices; quite as tho cheese tasting had something to do with the will of God; an idea he was to flee to the woods from like a noonday chimera. I knew there were deep and mean monastic politics grinding at him—he wasn't allergic to dairy products for nothing. His guts were, as they say, trying to say something to him. (They were also patient with him. I mean the monks, though several close early friendships soured and a few good friends wandered off. But one by one he gave up dreams for the Passion which the times thrust at him. It was a familiar pattern—honor and great name abroad, bad news at home.)

The greatness and goodness had something to do w. never refusing the next step by founding another think tank or Immobility Station. He started others off, and he was slower to see through principle to action, we must have understood how high a toll the country life exacted, as well as dogging bad health and loneliness. He was very much alone at the last years, in ways which are not normal or good—or in the original bargain—right seed, wrong flower. But he started something! I often have cause to reflect that in prison I have better facilities (in some ways) for reading, writing and prayer, than he had in the monastery, at least in the first years. Even in the 1st year in the woods he tore his back muscles splitting wood, froze and burned his bones at an open fireplace and was finally hospitalized once more. He sweated and froze it through: next winter they decreed a stove.

I guess it was his death taught me what death is all about. I suppose it always comes down to one person. A clogging of emotion & response, death stuck in the throat. Then the punched dough folds back and one finds himself upright again after all, though in a new and at times strange relationship to everyone: looking for a face, as though one's own.

Well here am I: in the sombres? I hope not, if he could be so ready, cool, feisty about the letting go, why not us as well? Same promise, same gift.

They tell me a parole appeal hearing is pending before Christmas. I go through the motions with my own accompaniment musically—mainly laughter up the sleeve. I fear I can never qualify the altitudinous moral requirements for rehab, refab or recycle. Must be that Jewish obsession with once & for all, move it! Exodus.

Thinking of you as we make advent. It is a good time, we will see it through. LOVE in all directions.

Daniel

(to our Mother)

7. THE FIRST CRY OF A CHILD

like an alert on a silent night
not merely signals from the void
I am here; things will never be the same.
this yes but more. For who can say
where the careening courses of the world will
impel him?

In the beginning
every son's mother rejoices
It is right and fitting
to rejoice
A child is born into the world.

It is fitting to rejoice also
in young manhood
"My sons have chosen well.
They have chosen honorably;
the priesthood honors them,
they honor its ranks."

Then change, change on the hour
that happy day
did not swallow them up inertly
they continued (alas and alleluia)
to choose, to be chosen.

In the first years they are unheard from
known to students, parishioners, friends:
peaceable, punctilious
They hold no great argument with the world
they walk in step with
ancestors, with posterity.

Only now and again it is noticed
they have a 3rd eye open
For bad news and good.

Days and nights, nights and days—
only a moratorium!
The third eye is the eye of a hurricane
the eye of a needle
(the world, the kingdom of God)

But what of parents (they see too, they
suffer)
Around that eye a storm gathers, a choice
contracts
hey too are listeners, they too take soundings;
'is his gift outright—is his substance equal
o the world's bluster, to the kingdom's coming?"

In face of such questions, they may
adopt one or another
expedient fearful heroic
response
e.g.—
Lacrymal—"You owe it to us not to—"
((breathe? see? taste? touch? move beyond?))
Reproving—"We have sacrificed everything—
surely you owe—"
Temporizing—"But no one else is so bedeviled—
maybe with time . . . things improve—"
OR—
OR—
Knowing that "old age" is a word coined by those who
never were young, to forbid moral aliveness
its promised staying heydey—
Shunting aside the body's weakness to reach out, to grip,
hand to hand to hand, the saving remnant—
those who march from life toward life
Dying out of death
gazing outward, inward with unflappable
Equanimity
Their lives a breathing consonance
With other lives, sons' and daughters' lives
Friends' lives, the lives of strangers,
Quick and unborn lives

WISHING
ALL WELL
WISHING ALL
WELL
WISHING ALL WELL

In a vital interactive interceding
Both passionate (we shall be judged by love)
And critical (we shall be judged)
So you come my dear
steering with matchless skill
Betwixt those monstrous obstacles
of good intent. I mean
SINKER AND CLINKER
Acedia and Bad Cess
Fear and Trembling
Nausea and Know Nothing
Spleen and Twice Seen

into the still waters
Bounded by Loretto Rest
and Danbury
and this May morning
1971
and our hands in yours
and our hearts in yours

Happy Mother's Day, dear—Daniel
Blessings, dear, and love—Phil

8. ON BEING HERE WITH PHIL

5/29/71

Whenever I met a crook here
    (con man, forger, break and entry, stocks and bonds)
I think gratefully
    as we pump damp hands
of Uncle Sam.

Strangely also of that dancing bear
who used on command
to heave himself up on slack legs
and flog about, an obscene pandemonium
like 5 men in a bear suit
up and down, rue Madame
in Paris, in '64.

Every day the gypsies would lead him out
chained at the neck
in a different scrap of costume—
a gypsy, a drunk, a clown
tatterdemalion, his rags tossed on him
    that A.M.
from ash cans or the Paris dump.

One and the same act, same moth-eaten bear.
You could see, if you wished to see
under the mask, the battered stovepipe hat
the fathomless liquid eyes, devoid
of terror or spirit. Eyes of a winded old horse
a cancer patient, a befuddled gypsy, a prisoner

This is what makes of pity a useful virtue.
I pump hands with the latest middle-age crook.
He played dominoes with Uncle Sam and lost.
Everyone loses: Rather—a sufficient number of suckers
to keep the game dangerous
with a public display of captive bears.

This one will dance here, 9 months or a year, a chain
dangling from his neck. (Lt. Strychnine
calling the dance) clothed like an animal
from the US Army dump.
Some call it
eating crow.

The crows laze overhead
like debris from the industry stack.
Day and night for slave wages
the prisoners make war instruments
to drop on Vietnamese peasants. This integrates
captive bears
with the "national effort."
The local shrinks in government hire
urge the prisoners into the factory
with psychological cattle prods.
Early parole is the reward
for bears who dance
as though their foot pads smoked
on hot coals.

The diet is crow.
Some go mad of it
One prisoner broke his chain
Climbed the water tower
befuddled, trying to catch crow
on the wing. Fellow bears
bellowed
obscene encouragement; jump you motherfucker

Sometimes (rarely, once or twice) pumping hands
with this or that crook, you see
flash out
not that old sodden look of defeat
but the game, the click, the authentic old
killer himself

the eyes of Uncle Sam.
(This is what makes of anger a useful virtue)

200 years old, about to celebrate
the bicentenary of his revolution.
The look of a war poster;
Uncle Sam Wants You

You're damned right he does.
The look goes through my body like a needle.
This one is no loser. This one
is light on his feet. The Russian bear
is yesterday's cub compared with this one.
Compared with this one
Your kind is practically extinct.
As to the future, any future
prisoners are advised to (do)
consult this one.

9. TULIPS IN THE PRISON YARD

All kinds of poets, believe me, could better praise your
sovereign beauty, your altogether subtle translation
of blank nature
So that winds, nights, sunlight
(extraordinarily colorless phenomena) are drawn into
What can only be called a "new game." Well I will not revel
in humiliation. Yeats, Wordsworth, would have looked once
Breathed deeply, gone home, sharpened quills,
with a flourish plucked you from time.
But
You are jailyard blooms, you wear bravery with a difference
You are born here, will die here. Making you, by excess of sufferin
And transfiguration of suffering, ours.
I see prisoners pass
In the dead spur of spring, before you show face.
Are you their glancing tears
The faces of wives and children,
the yin yang of hearts
To-fro like hanged necks,
in perpetual cruelty, absurdity?
The prisoners
Pass and pass, shades of men, pre-men, khaki ghosts; shame, futility
Between smiles, between reason for smiles, between
Life as fool's pace and life as celebrant's flame, is
Aeons.
Yet—thank you. Against the whips
of ignorant furies, the slavish pieties of Judas priests
You stand, a first flicker in the brain's soil, a precursor
of judgment—
Dawn might be
Man may be
Or spelling it out in the hand's palm
of a blind mute;
God is fire
is love

IV. Epilogue

[The following essay was written in 1969, after the death of David Darst, the youngest member of the Catonsville Nine. It is included here because of its relevance to all the preceding material.]

We Want Everyone to Fly. Come to Timeless, Peerless, FILETTO, to Quaint, Unspoiled *SONG MY*, or, if You Prefer, See America First. Come to Charming, Old World CATONSVILLE. Being a Memorial Celebration for David Darst.

We have been on the moon, and come back. We walk heavily where we used to leap, we barely jog where we used to run. And then tomorrow we say, and mean it (and we are right), who gives a damn about the moon any more? No one, but nothing, is obeying the law any more. The world is delivered over to poltergeists. The bread that used to break in our hands breaks in our faces. A Crazy Dog antipersonnel iron loaf.

David Darst burned draft files. David Darst died by fire. Who let the symbol loose? Didn't they know that fire is a wild fire, a raving beast? Cold comfort. Burning the papers in Catonsville, burned to death on the road. On his way to visit prisoners of conscience in jail. Someone pushed his own words in his face, a burning brand. And he died of it. Listen: *It is better to burn papers than children; it is better to die by fire than to kill by fire.* I know a few things about David, and I want to tell them, as far as grief permits.

He was a good man, in a classical sense. I mean to say, he dug deeper than the archeologists, he ranged further than the theologians. So he found, like Merton, how little sense it made to "leave one's order." No, he found a scene, he risked something, he put his life on a measurable line, he stood there while the cries of alarm rose and peaked—and then subsided. He did not seek enchantment in symbols, away from actual lives. He could not imagine, for all his beautiful and vital prowess and smile, ways of being human that were different from the ways his feet were proceeding on.

He was cheerful as pressures mounted. So he kept pushing the rest of us back to a time when we, too, were unbroken, and defeat was a mere word. I came to know something of this gift. David was ungalled. No one had strapped him in harness or shod him for drawing coals, with nails in his shoes, uphill to Newcastle—(the things most of us do, most of the time). No, his life was a gift. These days a gift is not a transformation, from an indentured clod into a prince of the earth. Or from a felon into a Jesuit Big Brother. No, the only gift worth giving is a simple lightening of a load beyond our bearing. In such wise that the cruel long haul goes virtually unnoticed. *Voilà* David! He whistled and sang, during all that week in jail while we fasted and grew new skins after Catonsville.

> "All, all come, all ascend, all come in, all sit down
> we were poor, poor, poor, poor, poor."
>
> (Zuni Indian Chant)

David was also the youngest of the Nine. His youth was a fact, a biology of the spirit. For us he was the first clue, that our intuitions stood within a history—that we had something to say that might quicken others. David came literally out of nowhere. He wrote Philip from St. Louis to say how moved he had been by the blood-pouring on draft files in November of 1967 in the Baltimore Customs House. And he wanted to come east to talk. His felonious leanings had a history; the vibrations, as they say, were good. David had previously sent back to their source, as violations of antiobscenity mailing laws, a series of the plastic hunting licenses that commonly go by the name of "draft cards." A real Christian, a real Brother! He was not trafficking in the indemnities of death. We used to kid him, delivered into God's right-hand pocket in the Baltimore County Jail. What a joke he had played on us; "A child shall lead them."

He was the most agile, unburdened, volatile, good-humored spirit in our neighborhood. He said: "I want to involve my part of the church in this protest." He was serious only by exception and interlude, under duress of law or judges of clerics. But his native air was that of a man who is—how else to say it—both Christian and Brother. Unburdened, new-born, free-wheeling extempore, alert, sensuous, a poetry machine, a self-destructing flower child. He smelled so much life around, he could never smell the death.

A bee, a flute with wings; the word was made of flowers: no garbage, no debris, no waste, no death. If you believed it, it came true, you transformed things. His life said, when one phase was over: *I live it and leave it; you may figure it out.*

He was also a Catholic. This belongs near the end of the catalog of his good points, because, like a poet or a poem, he tended to put the good things last; or even to leave them out entirely, except by indirection. It was a way of inviting others to a new kind of literacy. A Catholic; he loved the truth as it was given him to know it. The truth of things, the gift of God; it was his air, the ground under his feet. It might possibly be a crucial thing to be a Christian Brother, as it might be, in other circumstance, to be a Zen Buddhist, a Hasidic Jew, a guru of whatever stripe. (And with that I leave the subject of his faith, true to David's reticence and the metaphors he loved [literally] to fool around with, but never to perform autopsies upon.)

His Order didn't deserve him, that was a fact. But the fact was not something David was anxious to make much of. His Order had produced him, that was the real point. He was celibate, bright as quick silver, an easy rider, with no saddle sores. I conjure up his face, its bright, sharp, changeful planes, forever now beyond burning out, the arroyos and gullies which time and weather dig into a man. In his very brightness was all the pain and joy of being human today; but a *young* man! A face that, like a hardy perennial, is at its best when surrounded by others. Friendship: so much of the very point of living and of understanding life. David clones others in his own image, a feat of the spirit. (And there comes to me, incongruously, next to David's face, one of those heavy panhandled phizes of this or that theologian. Having looked on God [so they say] they turn men to stone. Faces that will sour a pan of innocent milk. "A man is responsible for his face.")

Mrs. Mary Church, a new bride blushing with her secrets, under the right moon (an ignorant nightingale celebrating outside, in Gregorian counterpoint) is made slow love to by J.C. Lord, her everloving, doomed, wounded, monogamous, magnanimous, virile, tender, blond, long-haired, blue-eyed, everloving, Only One. She conceives (oh, it's a miracle, by all accounts) a man-child. His coming makes a promised land. You know it. A little more essence and possibility, poured on the motor of things. For a day, while David is around, no one dies. No one dies! Please imagine it with me. Love seems logical, the mystery makes sense, the cruel riveted razor-edged conundrum falls apart and blows away. Logos at the heart of things.

ON NOT WAITING FOR THE TOMBSTONE CUTTER

He walked through an icy park at daybreak. The dead sat there like statuary, hunched in their coats and scarves, hating one another behind *The New York Times,* their eyeballs frozen to the perpetual bad news of this world. He went by, whistling in the graveyard. And the dead quickened, first in one bone, then another, as Jeremiah saw it. Frozen sticks, cast in a fire. They forgot death, the old filthy obituaries dropped from their hands (All the News Unfit to Print). They stood in shin bones, as we were meant to, they stood and tottered and felt their blood stirring like a thousand Saint Januariuses. They sucked in their breath from the sweet sharp air, they piped and squeaked, rusty as awakened bats; their voices warmed, they found a human scale again, they shouted, they exulted. They RAN after him, he beckoning them on; they jostled and milled around like a ragged Coxey's army, the eternal unemployed, on the move once more, something of value, in a people's park. It was the Seventh Seal he had opened. They all went off singing, off my screen, off today, off death. Forever. Cut.

We shall live again.
We shall live again.

(Comanche chant)

A problem for the FBI. How in the world will they arrange for the surrender of the person of defendant Darst to the marshals, to begin the serving of a sentence under the gentle aegis of the Federal Prison System? Will his ashes suffice? His flesh was reduced to a burnt offering in a fiery moment on the highway outside Omaha, that rainy night of October 30. He and two others were on their way to Waupan, Wisconsin, to visit the Milwaukee Fourteen, like David, guilty of the destruction of draft files. All three died.

Phoenix (fe-niks): a city. The capital of Arizona, on the Salt River, pop., 439,000. phoe-nix, phe-nix (fe-niks), n. (L. phoenix, fr. Gr. phoinix). In Egyptian mythology, a beautiful, lone bird which lived in the Arabian desert for 500 or 600 years and then consumed itself in fire, rising renewed from the ashes to start another long life; it is used as a symbol of immortality. (Webster)

The Darst motto: "Fight fire with fire." David interposed his body between the combustible flesh of children and the inflamed intentions of weapons' makers and improvers; all the American Krupps who traffic in human flesh. David found out; his flesh was combustible too.

The animal runs, it passes, it dies. And it is the great cold.
It is the great cold of the night, it is the dark.
The bird flies, it passes, it dies. And it is the great cold.
It is the great cold of the night, it is the dark.
The fish flees, it passes, it dies. And it is the great cold.
It is the great cold of the night, it is the dark.
Man eats and sleeps. He dies. And it is the great cold.
It is the great cold of the night, it is the dark.
There is light in the sky, the eyes are extinguished, the star shines.
The cold is below, the light is on high.
The man has passed, the shade has vanished, the prisoner is free!
Lord, Lord, come in answer to our call!
(Gabon death rites)

The storm was gathering around him for a year before Catonsville. In the summer of 1968 he was summoned to trial for refusing induction. With twenty-four hours to go, the government turned chicken, called off the hounds. Many of us had come to St. Louis in support of David, resigned to yet another weary farrago in court. We tried to say something to the church. For a day we circled the cathedral with pickets, during five hours of Sunday Masses. The stone hounds slept at the portals of the stone house, its people turned to stone. They came out, the Sunday votaries of the Cave of Plato, thousands of them, blinking in the sunlight. The strange, funky, rag-tag line of reality stood firm. We might as well have been Martians or yert dwellers. They stared and stared; it was a zoo, a circus; we were the first generation of "effete snobs." The Christians passed on.

Another day, in the same town, we had arranged to have a peace Mass. But the Jesuits nixed it; none of those outside hunkering agitators on their neat acres. And Jacqueline Grennin of Webster College ran for cover. So the peaceniks marched a mile or more along the central city, David at our head, a big crowd, a little church loaned to Roman DP's by the Protestant brethren. A good rap there, in the steaming Missouri night. Then, back for a party at the Christian Brothers' House.

It was an old arrangement, invariably a saving one. Everything we did led to a party. Someone even made a doctrine out of it: hold a party in order to plan a party. That kept it going, like the diurnity of God. And it comforted us to boot, as infallible dicta always do. And could those brothers run parties! Everybody in sight came, most of us brought strays. One night, at one party, I saw across the uproar, a priest–friend of auld lang syne, promoted since our last meeting to a big spot in the National Union. Well, well, said I to myself, let's see what gives. In a moment we were pumping hands like mad. I remembered him, from five years before, earnest, willful, unreamed. Some bishop's trouble spot, a tongue in a head, a brain, and a double dose of courage, a boiler-maker. Well, we sat down and shouted; there was nothing else to do; David's picket lines were subdued, but his parties were calliopes run amuck. My friend asked questions thick and fast. But something was wrong, you smelled it, somewhere in the meeting of eyes. The edge was off him, no malice and little humor, all that fine defenseless freedom gone. His eyes turned from an edgy hunter's to a spaniel's, concerned and somehow unconvincing. Several false starts; then I ventured something. When was the National Priest's Union going to speak up on the war, or offer a word of solidarity with the Catonsville felons? He leaned toward me, gathering steam. His hand was on my knee, a monsignor's tic.

Dan, just wait; in another year we'll have some political sock with the bishops, then you'll hear from us.

Another year come and gone. Sock, wham, pow, crash, the Priest's National Union beats away, unborn chicks with boxing gloves, pounding at the seamless egg. Celibacy, the vote, voice, salaries, the vernacular, celibacy, voice, etc., etc. The little victories add up to the big defeat. Now and again, mandarins of the first class consent to bargain with demi-mandarins. The war bleeds on. David Darst is dead. Mourn with me. And, the war, the war, the war goes on.

Some two years ago, a Jesuit superior said to me with considerable heat: "If only you would wait, until we have the difficulties in the Order settled, before bringing on these crises from outside!" I reposted mildly: "Could it be that the God of our Scripture, and presumably of our lives, might be urging a different timetable upon us? Like, how many deaths can you live with, in a house dedicated for the foreseeable future, to better housekeeping—and this, with children dying on the front lawn, in view of those safe in the house? What sort of picture can you bear at the picture window?"

I bring all this up, believe me, not out of addiction to the unpleasant, the bizarre, the cruel. I claim a bigger immunity from such a charge than even God can. To wit: not only did I not make the world, I have no hand in the way it goes. So God, I conclude, is innocent of complicity on one account alone, but I on both. Ha! No, I bring all this up because it is one way of approaching the gift of David Darst. During the year before Catonsville, he endured the dark night of the soul, the common lot of resisters. The bursar of the Christian brothers during that same year racked up, for the glory of God, a cold million on the stock market. A genius of sorts, such a charisma as to give pause to all but the most hardened of heart. David was apprised of this, from jail. Inevitably, a question arose. Would the brothers (Christian) syphon off some of the gravy for the liberation of their brother? You'd better believe not. It was in fact the usual long-haired, blond, blue-eyed, resisting agitators who scraped the bread together to get their brother sprung. Crumbs, so to speak, of Lazarus, off Midas' table.

A question therefore arises: Who, on what day, will leap the chasm set eternally between Lazarus and Midas, a drop of water intact in the palm of the long-distance runner, to assuage the fire that racks his brother, damned to hell?

This is about David. He could not live with death. He had no bargaining skills. He had no diamond merchant's scales, fine to the hair's breadth. He was no moral theologian. He came upon no reason to leave his scene, to leave his work, to leave his Order, or his family. His inventive guts, prophetic as Hamlet's, told him something else. It was an oracle for those who could travel fast and free, and still never leave home. Come to Catonsville!

He came to Catonsville. He believed the martyrs, he trusted the virgins, he shared his secrets with the confessors, he dug Gandhi, he was into Chairman Jesus and his quotations. David was his own diamond scale, delicate as diamond, I saw it in his eyes, and rejoiced.

How do you deal with your life? There are at least as many ways of dying as there are of living. David, for his part, could have lived in that middle ground of partying, study, female-fluttering, sacred and secular bread and circuses that make up the lives of so many clerics today. No great loss, no great gain. But something else happened to him; by what intervention who can say? We only know that he was young enough of heart, lucid enough of spirit, long enough of reach, to come on a certain yardstick. He put the rod against the common life of man today, and drew it back. And he saw something better than the *horror vacui* of the middle years. He saw that the measuring rod was stained with blood. "The bloodstained face of history today." He was, from that moment, lost.

I want to take something back if I have said too much. For I do not want to make too much of him. There is a way of inflating the dead, their uniqueness, their stature, simply because one is a writer of sorts, and the friend of a writer must therefore be "of import." David was in many ways a conventional man. He sat in backyards for the unchanging summer rites of suburbia. In religion he was Roman, in politics, as far as I know, a rather excitable Whig. His *Weltanschauung* was tempered by his sense of original sin. Change might be on the way, but nothing could quite equal or translate or nullify those passages of Scripture which spoke of the shaking of foundations, the recurrent corruption of power, the hankering after slaveries, the dominion (all but universal, all but conceded) of death.

A miser is one who wrings the neck of the world, forces its essence out, into a wineskin. In some such way, I tasted the quality of David—the fine muscatel of the world, a good vintage. A good year—1968, year of growth; 1969, the pressing and bottling.

A year before David's death thousands of people his age gathered in Chicago to combat the creeping death-dealing foulness of the public scene. Weeks before his death came the incredible massing of the tribes at Woodstock. The best of their generation surface, in the main, for one of two reasons: (1) to celebrate the creation of a subculture (the politics of alienation); (2) to disrupt the chilling routine of business as usual, death as usual (the politics of contempt). The rest of us are free to read and run as we will: to raise an outcry, to listen in dread or in hope, to try out eyes and reflexes at a local shooting gallery, a Doberman pinscher rental agency, or a local draft board. Some leave America, some stay to pollute it; and some hang around at the edges, their bodies chilled by the dissipation of a once great hope. What a marvelous century it might have been. Imagine what we might have done with our lives!

"I flew out to Baltimore the night before, May 16, to get some sleep before the action. But we didn't get much sleep that night." No, indeed. You don't get much sleep the night before a birth or a death. We were stuck with one of the other event, we still don't know which. But we are sure beyond serious doubt that what happened on May 17, 1968, wasn't a mere reshuffling of an old deck, a scrutiny of limp entrails, a carving of cold turkey. No, it was something more. Something died, something got born. That's so simple an event you can speak of it to children, or even allow it to happen to yourself.

As I set this down, two more days of the hunting season remain. Then I can put away the Day-Glo personnel anti-hunter's vest; stenciled on its back: "I am a man. Don't shoot."

Ten thousand miles away, a village massacre. Here, you can't hear a thing, not a shot, not a scream. In jails, crazy houses, supermarkets, bedrooms, hash joints, fruit stands, you can't hear a thing. Live in the heart of the pomegranate, eat the seeds which induce forgetfulness.

The judge said to David and the rest of us: "We can always affect policies, write our congressman. But those who break the law must expect to be punished." Indeed.

The testimony of David Darst, at the trial of the Catonsville Nine;

> I was not in the room
> when the files were taken
> Perhaps I could be called
> the lookout man
> If anyone came to stop us
> I was to hurry in
> and let the others know
> One might have called it
> a Bonnie and Clyde act
> on behalf of God and man

D. Do you recall the substance with which the records were burned?

> They were burned with a kind of a crude napalm
> We made it from a formula
> in the Special Forces Handbook
> published by the School for Special Warfare
> at Fort Bragg

We did not use all the ingredients called for
We made a very crude form of napalm
consisting of two parts gasoline
one part soap flakes
Nor did we cook our mix into a jelly
We left it in liquid form
so we could pour it on the files
We felt it was fitting that this agent
which had burned human flesh
in the war in Vietnam and in many other places
should now be poured on the records
which gave war and violence
such abstract legitimacy

D. Would you explain your intent in acting at Catonsville, other than destroying the files?

First of all to raise a cry
an outcry at what was clearly a crime
an unnecessary suffering
a clear and wanton slaughter
Perhaps this is similar to the case
of a man in his home who sees a crime
someone is being attacked outside
His impulse I think his
basic human impulse
is to cry out to call for help
That was one intention
an outcry that hopefully
would stop the crime
I saw being perpetrated
Another intention was
to halt the machine of death
which I saw moving and killing
In the same way perhaps
a person in Czechoslovakia
when tanks invade his country
throws bricks into the wheels
of the tanks
and sometimes a puny effort

stops a tank
This was my hope
to hinder this war
in a literal way
an actual physical way

D. Do you have any other basis for the intent you have described?

An outcry against the fact
that our country can spend
eighty billions a year
chasing imaginary enemies
all around the world
I was living last year
in a poor ghetto district
I saw many little children
who did not have enough to eat
This is a very moving thing
Our country
cannot summon enough energy
to give bread and milk
to children
Yet it can rain fire and death
on people ten thousand miles away
for reasons that are unclear
to most thoughtful men

D. Did your religious belief have any influence on your decision?

Well I suppose my thinking
is part of an ethic
found in the New Testament
I suppose you could say
Jesus too was guilty
of assault and battery
when he cast the moneychangers
out of the temple
and wasted their property and wealth
He was saying
It is wrong to do what you are doing
And this was our point

We came to realize
draft files are death's own cry
We have not been able
to let sacred life
and total death
live together quietly within us
We have cried out on behalf of life
The government has chosen
to see our cry
as anarchy and arrogance
But the acts of men and women
who turn themselves in for jail sentences
will not inspire others to such anarchy
Perhaps real anarchy lies
in the acts of those who
have ravaged war upon a proud people
in the face of a great and burning doubt
This doubt cries to heaven
Our cry too goes out
in the name of life
Men around the world hear and take heart
We are one with them We believe that today
we are at a joyful beginning We are together
and we are not afraid

All. When the storm has growled
Leader. They await him who will come
All. Him who will come
Leader. Him who will say; you come
All. Him who will say; come
Leader. And God will be with his sons
All. With his sons
And this is the end
(from a Gabon chant)

December 5, 1969

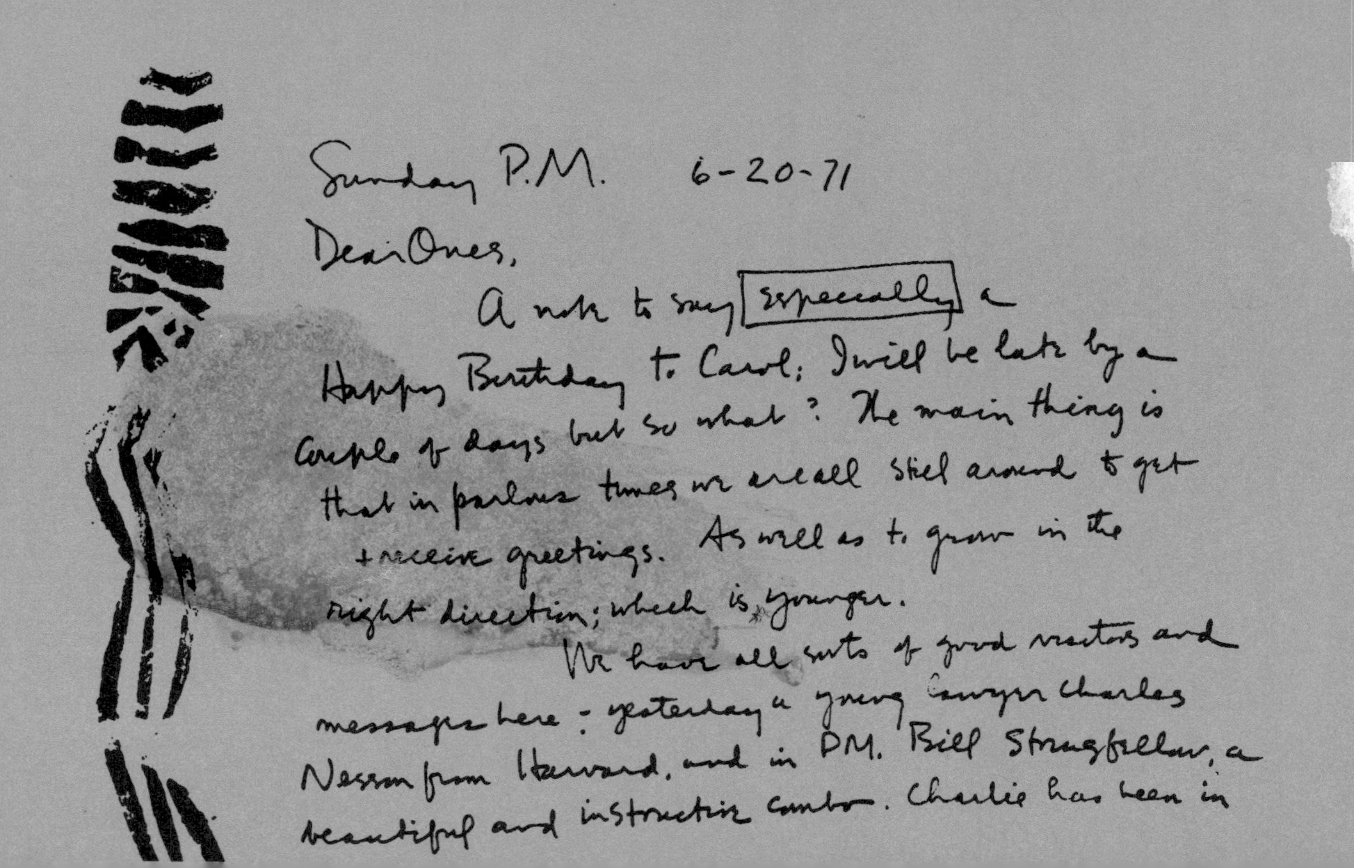

Sunday P.M. 6-20-71

Dear Ones,

A note to say [especially] a
Happy Birthday to Carol; I will be late by a
couple of days but so what? The main thing is
that in parlous times we are all still around to get
+ receive greetings. As well as to grow in the
right direction; which is younger.

We have all sorts of good visitors and
messages here: yesterday a young lawyer Charles
Nesson from Harvard, and in P.M. Bill Stringfellow, a
beautiful and instructive combo. Charlie has been in